CW00918994

WINDY DRYDE

WINDY DRYDEN LIVE!

Windy Dryden

Rationality Publications

Rationality Publications
136 Montagu Mansions, London W1U 6LQ

www.rationalitypublications.com
info@rationalitypublications.com

First edition published by Rationality Publications
Copyright (c) 2021 Windy Dryden

A catalogue record of this book is
available from the British Library.

First edition 2021

ISBN: 978-1-910301-95-1

Contents

Preface

The focus of this book is the brief online REBT sessions I do with volunteers for the 'REBT Facebook Group'[1] established and run by Matt Walters. Matt set up the group on 2 June 2018 to create a place where members of the group can find a vast array of information on REBT in one online space. The group caters for everyone from those new to REBT to established practitioners and REBT academics. At the time of writing, it has almost 7,000 members.

I agreed to run weekly, one-hour, brief REBT demonstrations for the group, and we held our first session on 20 October 2020. The chosen time (3pm–4pm UK time on Mondays) allows people in Europe and India to watch the demonstrations and volunteer. We have called the sessions 'Windy Dryden Live!' because I am conducting them, and I am doing so 'live'.

In the live broadcast, I do either two or three demonstrations. Matt finds the volunteers for me, whom he briefs in advance. Once I have finished a conversation, Matt moderates the questions for me from the online audience. The conversations are not available for later review.

In Part I of the book, I begin by giving a brief outline of REBT in Chapter 1, and in Chapter 2 I discuss my work in these short REBT-based conversations. Then in Part II of the book, in Chapters 3–15, I present the transcripts of 13 of these conversations with commentary to give readers a sense of what can be achieved with REBT in a short period. These sessions range from 10 minutes 49 seconds to 25 minutes 33 seconds, the average being 17 minutes 14 seconds.

I want to thank the volunteers for agreeing to let me publish the transcripts of our conversations in this book. The volunteers themselves have selected the names that appear in the discussions.

---

[1] www.facebook.com/groups/960282217430295/

I hope each volunteer has taken away something of value from our conversation that they can implement in their life. I also hope that you, dear reader, will find the book instructive and that you will soon join Matt and me at 'Windy Dryden Live!'.

Windy Dryden
London & Eastbourne
June 2021

PART I

FOUNDATIONS

1

The Theory of Rational Emotive Behaviour Therapy (REBT): In Brief

In this opening chapter, I will summarise the information you will need to know about to make sense of the conversations that I present in Chapters 3–15.

A modified version of Epictetus's famous dictum[2] explains REBT's position on psychological disturbance: 'People disturb themselves by holding rigid and extreme attitudes[3] towards life's adversities.' REBT's position on psychological health is as follows: 'People respond healthily to life's adversities when they hold flexible and non-extreme attitudes[4] towards them.' I outline these respective attitudes in Table 1.1.

Ellis (1983) argued that rigid attitudes are at the very core of psychological disturbed responses to adversities and that extreme attitudes are derived from this rigid attitudinal core. Similarly, flexible attitudes are at the very core of psychologically healthy responses to adversities and non-extreme attitudes are derived from this flexible attitudinal core. Table 1.1 shows these points graphically.

1.1 The components of rigid and flexible attitudes

As many of the conversations in this book show, when I assess a person's rigid attitude towards an adversity, I also assess their flexible attitude at the same time. This is because both

---

[2] 'Men are disturbed not by things but by their views of things.'
[3] I use the terms 'rigid/extreme attitudes' rather than 'irrational beliefs' for reasons that I explain in Dryden (2016).
[4] I use the terms 'flexible/non-extreme attitudes' rather than 'rational beliefs' for reasons that I again explain in Dryden (2016).

attitudes have a shared component and differentiating components (see Table 1.2).

Table 1.1   Rigid and extreme attitudes vs flexible and non-extreme attitudes

Rigid attitudes	Flexible attitudes
↓	↓
Extreme attitudes	**Non-extreme attitudes**
• Awfulising attitudes	• Non-awfulising attitudes
• Unbearability attitudes	• Bearability attitudes
• Devaluation attitudes	• Unconditional acceptance attitudes

Table 1.2 The components of rigid and flexible attitudes

Rigid attitude	Flexible attitude
Preference [Shared component] *'I want to do well...*	Preference [Shared component] *'I want to do well...*
Asserted demand [Differentiating component] *...and therefore I have to do well'*	Negated demand [Differentiating component] *....but I don't have to do well'*

1.2 The components of awfulising attitudes and non-awfulising attitudes

When I assess a person's awfulising attitude towards an adversity, I also assess their non-awfulising attitude at the same time. Again, this is because both attitudes have a shared component and differentiating components (see Table 1.3).

Table 1.3 The components of awfulising and non-awfulising attitudes

Awfulising attitude	Non-awfulising attitude
Evaluation of badness [Shared component] *'It is bad if I don't do well...*	Evaluation of badness [Shared component] *'It is bad if I don't do well...*
Asserted awfulising [Differentiating component] *...and therefore it is awful if I don't do well'*	Negated awfulising [Differentiating component] *...but it is not awful if I don't do well'*

1.3 The components of unbearability attitudes and bearability attitudes[5]

Again, when I assess a person's unbearability attitude towards an adversity, I also assess their bearability attitude at the same time. As before, this is because both attitudes have a shared component and differentiating components (see Table 1.4).

---

[5] I prefer the terms 'unbearability' and 'bearability' to 'discomfort intolerance' and 'discomfort tolerance' or 'low frustration tolerance' and 'high frustration tolerance' because unlike the other two sets of terms the aforementioned terms do not specify an adversity (e.g. discomfort or frustration). This brings it in line with the other three sets of attitudes which also do not specify an adversity.

Table 1.4 The components of unbearability and bearability attitudes

Unbearability attitude	Bearability attitude
Struggle [Shared component] *'Not doing well is difficult to bear...*	Struggle [Shared component] *'Not doing well is difficult to bear...*
Asserted unbearability [Differentiating component] *...and therefore I can't bear it if I don't do well'*	Asserted bearability [Differentiating component] *...but I can bear it if I don't do well...* Worth it [Differentiating component] *....It is worth it to me to bear not doing well...* Willingness [Differentiating component] *...I am willing to bear not doing well...* Commitment [Differentiating component] *...and I commit myself to bear it...* Taking action [Differentiating component] *...and I am taking action to bear it'.*

1.4 The components of devaluation attitudes and unconditional acceptance attitudes

There are three objects of devaluation and unconditional acceptance attitudes: self, other(s) or life/life conditions. Yet again when I assess a person's devaluation in the face of an adversity, I also assess their unconditional acceptance attitude at the same time. As before, this is because both attitudes have a shared component and differentiating components (see Table 1.5). I will illustrate this with reference to self-devaluation and unconditional self-acceptance attitudes.

Table 1.5 The components of devaluation and unconditional acceptance attitudes

Devaluation attitude	Unconditional acceptance attitude
Negatively evaluated aspect [Shared component] *'Not doing well is bad ...*	Negatively evaluated aspect [Shared component] *'Not doing well is bad ...*
Asserted devaluation (of self/others/life) [Differentiating component] *... and therefore I am worthless'*	Negated devaluation (of self/others/life) [Differentiating component] *... but that does not mean that I am worthless...*
	Asserted unconditional acceptance (of self/others/life) [Differentiating component] *... It means that I am a fallible human being who did not do well on this occasion but I am capable of doing well, doing OK and not doing well'*

1.5 The differential consequences of holding rigid/extreme attitudes and flexible/non-extreme attitudes

I mentioned at the beginning of this chapter REBT's views on psychological disturbance and health in a nutshell. These are:

- 'People respond in a disturbed way to life's adversities when they hold rigid and extreme attitudes towards them.

- People respond healthily to life's adversities when they hold flexible and non-extreme attitudes towards them.

In this section, I will amplify on these two dictums. Table 1.6 presents the differential emotional, behavioural and thinking consequences of holding rigid/extreme and flexible/non-extreme attitudes respectively.

1.6 Unhealthy negative emotions (UNEs) and healthy negative emotions (HNEs)

It is important to note that REBT is unique among approaches to CBT in distinguishing between unhealthy and healthy negative emotions. An unhealthy negative emotion (UNE) is an emotion with a negative feeling tone, which has largely unconstructive effects. A healthy negative emotion (HNE) also has a negative feeling tone, but has largely constructive effects. This means that it is healthy for a person to feel bad when holding a flexible/non-extreme adversity towards an adversity. Thus, an REB therapist will intervene when a person wants to set an emotional goal where they want to feel:

- A less intense version of a UNE (e.g. 'I want to feel less anxious'). Such an emotion is still unhealthy and still sends from a rigid/extreme attitude.
- An absence of a UNE (e.g. 'I don't want to feel anxious'). People do not live in an emotional vacuum and it is more constructive for a person to feel an HNE than a UNE.
- Indifferent, calm or 'OK'. These states ignore the fact that the person prefers the adversity to be absent and when it is present they are going to feel negatively about it. Given this their choice is to experience a UNE or an HNE.

Table 1.6 The differential emotional, behavioural and thinking consequences of holding rigid/extreme and flexible/non-extreme attitudes

Adversity ↓	Adversity ↓
Rigid/extreme attitudes ↓	Flexible/non-extreme attitudes ↓
Consequences 1. Emotional (unhealthy negative) • Anxiety • Depression • Guilt • Shame • Hurt • Unhealthy anger • Unhealthy jealousy • Unhealthy envy 2. Behavioural • Unconstructive • Self-defeating • Relationship-defeating 3. Thinking • Highly distorted and negatively skewed • Ruminative	Consequences 1. Emotional (healthy negative) • Concern • Sadness • Remorse • Disappointment • Sorrow • Healthy anger • Healthy jealousy • Healthy envy 2. Behavioural • Constructive • Self-enhancing • Relationship-enhancing 3. Thinking • Balanced • Non-ruminative

1.7 A negative emotion suggests what adversity the person is facing

One of the most important tasks that the REB therapist has in the assessment process is to help the person to identify the adversity that features in their problem. I will outline the method I use to do this in Chapter 2. What I will do here is to present in Table 1.7, a list of the eight major unhealthy negative emotions (UNEs) for which people seek therapeutic help, and their healthy emotional alternatives (HNEs) and, most importantly for our current purpose, the major adversities that are associated with both sets of negative emotions.

This table indicates a number of points:

1. An adversity does not cause an emotion. Rather when a person holds a rigid/extreme attitude towards an adversity they will experience a UNE and when they hold a flexible/non-extreme attitude towards the same adversity they will experience an HNE (see Table 1.7)
2. The same adversity is present in a person's emotional problem and in the solution to this problem
3. We can use either an UNE or an HNE to identify an adversity

In this chapter, I have presented the ABC framework that REB therapists use in their practice and which informs my work in the brief conversations that I do for the REBT Facebook Group. At, 'A', I outlined the major adversities that feature in people's emotional problems, at 'B' I outlined the four major basic rigid/extreme attitudes that underpin these emotional problems and the four alternative flexible/non-extreme attitudes that provide the attitudinal solutional to these problems. In doing so, I outlined the shared and differentiating components of these two sets of basic attitudes at 'B'. Finally, at 'C', I outlined the differential consequences of holding both sets of attitudes. In the next chapter, I will outline the main features of my REBT practice in the very brief conversations that are the focus for this book.

Table 1.7 Adversities with associated unhealthy and healthy negative emotions

Adversity	Negative Emotion	
	Unhealthy	Healthy
• Threat	Anxiety	Concern
• Loss • Failure • Undeserved plight (experienced by self or others)	Depression	Sadness
• Breaking your moral code • Failing to abide by your moral code • Hurting someone	Guilt	Remorse
• Falling very short of your ideal in a social context • Others judging you negatively	Shame	Disappointment
• The other is less invested in your relationship than you • Someone betrays you or lets you down and you think do not deserve such treatment	Hurt	Sorrow
• You or another transgresses a personal rule • Another disrespects you • Frustration	Unhealthy anger	Healthy anger
• Someone poses a threat to a valued relationship • You experience uncertainty related to this threat	Unhealthy jealousy	Healthy jealousy
• Others have what you value and lack	Unhealthy envy	Healthy envy

2

Using REBT in Brief Therapeutic Conversations: The Main Features of My Practice

Imagine that you have only up to 25 minutes to help somebody with their emotional problem. What would you do? In this chapter I will discuss my answer to this question and in Part II I will present 13 transcripts of conversations that I have had with volunteers under the 'Windy Dryden Live!' banner for the REBT Facebook Group to show my approach in action.

2.1 Beginning the conversation

Each volunteer for these live online conversations is briefed for the session by Matt Walters, the co-ordinator of the REBT Facebook Group. However, as I have not been a party to this briefing, I want to make sure that the volunteer and I are on the same page concerning the conversation that we are about to have. Consequently, the most common way I initiate the conversation with the volunteer is to ask them for their understanding of its purpose (e.g. 'What is your understanding of the purpose of our conversation today?'). Of the 13 conversations included in this book, I began the session in this way on 9 occasions. In two instances, I asked the person for their problem, on one instance, I asked the person how they wanted to send the time we have together and on one other instance I asked the person what they hoped to achieve from the conversation. So, in the vast majority of cases, I ask a focusing question to begin: on purpose, problem or goal.

2.2 Being and remaining focused

In such a short conversation, it is important that the volunteer and myself select a focus and keep to this focus. This will almost always be a problem with which the person is currently struggling. My brief to Matt Walters is to find volunteers who have a current problem for which they would like help and that they do not mind discussing in front of an online audience united by their interest in REBT. Thus, the volunteer will have had an opportunity to think about which problem that would like to discuss with me. Once we have agreed to focus on a problem, which I refer to as the person's 'nominated' problem, it is largely my responsibility to help us both keep to this focus.

2.3 Being goal-directed

In these conversations, I am mindful of the importance of helping the person take away something meaningful that they can implement in their life. To this end, it is important to know where the person and I are headed in the conversation. This involves me asking the person about their goal. There are two types of goals that can be set in these conversations: a session goal – what the person wants to walk away with from the session – and a problem-related goal – what the person wants to achieve related to their goal. Ideally, achieving the session goal will be a step in the right direction towards the resolution of the person's problem.

   I am especially interested in helping the person set and work towards experiencing a healthy negative emotion in the face of the adversity that features in their problem since this is in line with REBT theory as discussed in Chapter 1.

2.4 Assessing the problem

Assessing the person's problem accurately is, in my view, a very important therapist task in very brief REBT. Indeed, I would say that I devote most of my time doing this in these conversations

2.4.1 Identifying the UNE

Identifying the person's major UNE is usually the first task in assessing the person's problem. Often this is clear, but when I am unsure whether the emotion is a UNE or and HNE, I use the person's accompanying behaviour and thinking to help me in this respect.

2.4.2 Identifying the main adversity in the person's problem

Again, identifying the person's 'A' is sometimes straightforward; however, when it is not I use 'Windy's Magic Question' (WMQ) to help me (see Table 2.1).

Table 2.1 Windy's Magic Question (WMQ)

Purpose: To help the volunteer to identify the 'A' in the ABC framework as quickly as possible (i.e. what the person is most disturbed about) once 'C' has been assessed and the situation in which 'C' has occurred has been identified and briefly described. I take the following steps.

- I have the person focus on their disturbed 'C' (e.g. 'anxiety')
- I then ask the person to focus on the situation in which 'C' occurred (e.g. 'about to give a public presentation to my peer group')
- I then ask the person: *'Which ingredient could we give you to eliminate or significantly reduce "C"'?* (here, anxiety). (In this case the person said: 'my mind not going blank'). I take care that the person does not change the situation (i.e. they do not say: 'not giving the presentation')
- The opposite is probably 'A' (e.g. 'my mind going blank'), but I usually check and ask: *'So when you were about to give the presentation, were you most anxious about your mind going blank?'* If not, I use the question again until the person confirms what they were most anxious about in the described situation

2.4.3 Identifying attitudes

After I have assessed the person's 'C' and 'A', I am ready to help them to identify the rigid/extreme attitudes that underpin their problem and at the same time the flexible/non-extreme attitudes that underpin the solution to this problem. I do this by using what I term 'Windy's Review Assessment Procedure' (WRAP) (see Table 2.2).

2.5 Examining attitudes

Once I have helped the person to identify both sets of attitudes. I help them to examine these attitudes to determine which attitude they would like to take further. In this, I am guided by a way of examining attitudes that I have called, 'Windy's Choice-Based Method of Examining Attitudes' (see Table 2.3). In a brief conversation, I will use elements of this way of helping a person to examine their attitudes rather than the whole of this approach

2.6 Rehearsing the attitudinal solution

REBT favours attitudinal solutions to emotional problems and in the above section, I outlined how this work can be implemented in brief REBT-based conversations. Once such a solution has been selected by the person, I will encourage them to rehearse it. This could involve them imagining themself acting in a way that is consistent with their selected flexible/non-extreme attitude, using roleplay to practice the attitude in a simulated situation or through some kind of chairwork.

Table 2.2 Windy's Review Assessment Procedure (WRAP)

Purpose: I have assessed 'C' (e.g. 'anxiety') and 'A' (e.g. 'my mind going blank'), I use this technique to identify both the volunteer's rigid and alternative flexible attitude and to help the client to understand the two relevant B-C connections. This technique can also be used with any of the derivatives of the rigid and flexible attitude belief pairing.

- I begin by saying, *'Let's review what we know and what we don't know so far.'*
- I then say, *'We know three things. First, we know that you were anxious ("C"). Second, we know that you were anxious about your mind going blank ("A"). Third, and this is an educated guess on my part, we know that it is important to you that your mind does not go blank. Am I correct?'* Assuming that the person confirms my hunch, note that what I have done is to identify the part of the attitude that is common to both the person's rigid attitude and alternative flexible attitude, as we will see.
- Next, I say: *'Now let's review what we don't know. This is where I need your help. We don't know which of two attitudes your anxiety was based on. So, when you were anxious about your mind going blank was your anxiety based on Attitude 1: "It is important to me that my mind does not go blank and therefore it must not do so"* ('Rigid attitude') *or Attitude 2: "It is important to me that my mind does not go blank, but that does not mean that it must not do so"* ('Flexible attitude')?'
- If necessary, I help person to understand that their anxiety was based on their rigid attitude if they are unsure.
- Once the person is clear that their anxiety was based on their rigid attitude, I make and emphasize the rigid attitude-disturbed 'C' connection. Then, I ask: *'Now let's suppose instead that you had a strong conviction in attitude 2, how would you feel about your mind going blank if you strongly believed that while it was important to you that your mind did not go blank, it did not follow that it must not do so?'*
- If necessary, I help the person to nominate a healthy negative emotion such as concern, if not immediately volunteered, and make and emphasize the flexible attitude-healthy 'C' connection.
- I ensure that the person clearly understands the differences between the two B-C connections.
- Then, I help the person set concern as the emotional goal in this situation and encourage them to see that developing conviction in their flexible attitude is the best way of achieving this goal.

Table 2.3 Windy's Choice-Based Method of Examining Attitudes: instructions for use

- I ask the person to focus their rigid attitude and their flexible attitude[a]
- Then, I ask the person which attitude is true and which is false and to give reasons for their choice
- Next, I ask them which attitude is logical and which illogical false and to give reasons for their choice
- Next, I ask them attitude is helpful and which unhelpful and to give reasons for their choice
- Following on from the above, I ask the person which attitude they would teach their children and to give reasons for their choice
- Then, I ask them to which attitude they wish to commit themself going forward and to give reasons for their choice
- Finally, I ask the person to voice any doubts, reservations they have about their decision and I deal with their responses

[a] These instructions can also be used when asking the person to examine any extreme/non-extreme attitude pairing.

2.7 Moving beyond the conversation

Before ending the session, where possible, it is important that I encourage the person to implement what they have learned from the conversation in their everyday life and, if relevant, to identify and deal with any obstacles to doing so.

2.8 How I am influenced by single-session thinking in these conversations

I see the brief REBT-based conversations that I have with volunteers as a form of single-session therapy. Consequently, in addition to the REBT ideas that ideas and techniques that I have discussed in this chapter and the previous one, I am also influenced by some aspects of single-session thinking (Hoyt, Young and Rycroft, 2021). In this session I will briefly mention some of these influences. It is important for me to make clear that I will not act on all these influences in any given session. Rather, just like a handyperson who carries around them with a toolbox not knowing which tools they may need on a particular job, I will use those SST-based tools as and when they are needed.

2.8.1 Utilise the person's strengths and values

When I have a brief conversation based on REBT with a volunteer I draw upon what REBT has to offer me and what the client has to offer themself. In this latter respect, I encourage the person to identify those strengths and values that they have and which they think will help them as they work towards addressing their emotional problem.

2.8.2 Utilise the person's external resources

In addition to their internal resources, I sometimes encourage the person to identify resources that are available to them in their environmental that can help the to solve their problems. These resources may include people who can provide assistance and support to the person, organisations that may offer some kind of aid and relevant self-help material and phone/computer 'apps'.

2.8.3 Experience of solving the same or similar problems

It is possible that the person may already have had the experience of solving their problem or similar problems. If so, I will help the person to see that they can use the helpful ingredients of these success experiences and apply them to their nominated problem.

2.8.4 Learning from failed attempts to solve the problem

The person has probably made a number of attempts to solve their nominated problem and much can be gained from understanding what the person has done and why these attempts failed. This can lead to a useful discussion of what alternative problem-solving strategies the person can use. Often these include the opposite of the strategies that failed.

Now that I have outlined how I approach helping a volunteer in a 'Windy Dryden Live!' session, in Part II of this book I present 13 transcripts of actual conversations that I have had with volunteers together with my commentary on salient points from each conversation.

PART II

THE CONVERSATIONS

3

Helping the Person to Tell Her Clients about Her Professional Charges

Windy–Lata: Interview on 11/01/21
Length: 18 minutes 18 secs

Windy: OK, so, we have 25 minutes together to have a conversation. What do you hope to achieve from our conversation?

Lata: I hope to get out of the mental blockage that I have right now, at the end of this conversation.

Windy: So, at the moment you're in some kind of mental blockage and you need the services of a therapeutic plumber.

[Single-session therapy is particularly useful to help people get unstuck or in this case deal with 'blockages'. My reference to me being a 'therapeutic plumber' illustrates my use of humour in single-session work.]

Lata: Yeah, this particular mental blockage.

Windy: OK, good. Please tell me about the blockage?

Lata: Yeah. So, I'm a counselling psychologist myself and I find it very difficult to tell about my charges to the clients.

Windy: Right. So, you charge them fees?

Lata: Yes.

Windy: So, what do you do? Do you see them for free?

Lata: No. I started doing for free and then I realised I'm finding it difficult to pay my bills.

Windy: That's correct. Of course, you're getting this free. You realise that?

Lata: Yes.

Windy: So, what do you charge, if you don't mind telling the world?

Lata: Yes. I charge rupees 1500 per session.

Windy: 1500 rupees per session. Now, do you know what that is in sterling?

Lata: It would be around… [*pause*], I don't know. I'll have to calculate it.

[*It is about £15.*]

Windy: Alright. Do you know other people in your position charging around the same or do they charge more or do they charge less?

Lata: There are many people who charge more and I would say few people charging less. Most of them charge more than I charge.

Windy: So, do you also have a problem charging correctly or are you happy with what your charges are?

Lata: I'm happy with the amount that I'm charging right now.

Windy: OK. So, erm, how would you like to tell people what your charges are? At what point in the process?

Lata: … [*pause*] So, I would like to tell them that I charge rupees 1500 per session.

Windy: You want to tell them face to face or what?

Lata: Right now, since everything has moved onto either a phone call or Zoom, yeah, I would like to tell them in the first instance because then it becomes easier for them to take a decision, but I hold myself back.

[*I have been working to get a sense of how Lata sees the problem and what she wants to achieve.*]

Windy: OK. So, what's your own view about why you hold yourself back?

Lata: OK, the first thought that comes into my mind is that would they be ready to pay more than are they able to pay. It's just would they be ready to pay – that's my first question to myself.

Windy: What do you mean by 'ready'? They are able, you mean they can afford it, but, by 'ready', what do you mean by 'ready'?

Lata: Would they be willing to pay 1500.

Windy: Be willing, OK. I don't know. So, that's not stopping you because you could say, 'Would they be willing? I don't know.'

Lata: Right.

Windy: Right. Unless you'd like a guarantee that they would be willing. Is that what you're looking for, a guarantee?

Lata: No. There would be no guarantee.

Windy: OK. So, that doesn't explain why you're holding yourself back.

Lata: … Right, that doesn't explain.

Windy: No.

Lata: I'll give you an example, if it's OK to give?

[I was about to ask Lata for an example when she suggested it herself.]

Windy: Please do.

Lata: Recently, I did a counselling session, in fact the first time the mother called it was for a child, so, when the mother called, I managed to tell her my fee and then, towards the end of the conversation, she asked, 'Oh, would you reduce your fee a little bit?' so that put me in a very uncomfortable situation. So, this is something that plays on my mind: if they say that, how do I respond?

Windy: Well, I guess your choices are what?

Lata: … Right.

Windy: What are your choices?

[I often ask a person in SST what their choices or options are because doing so helps to clarify matters and suggests to the person that they have agency in choosing among alternatives.]

Lata: My choices are either I say, 'Yes,' and reduce the charge, or I say, 'No,' and I stick to my... charges.

Windy: And what do you want to do?

Lata: I want to stick to my charges.

Windy: So, how are you stopping yourself from doing that?

Lata: Again, there is something inside me telling, 'Will they come back for the session? Would they take the session from you?'

Windy: Yeah. And, again, what's the answer to that?

Lata: Nothing.

Windy: What's the feeling that goes along with this block, because, whenever there's a block – in other words, you want to go there and you're here, and you want to go there but there's a feeling that's associated with you stopping from going there – what's the feeling that's associated with the block?

[I am now assessing the person's problem and begin by helping her to identify the feeling associated with the block.]

Lata: The feeling is... *[pause]* kind of an inadequacy.

Windy: Well, that's not a feeling, but we'll go along with that. You've got feelings of inadequacy. You mean of inadequacy as a psychologist or inadequacy as a person?

[A feelings of inadequacy, as I point out to Lata, in not an emotion, but I can work with it as such. Note that I also ask whether her sense of inadequacy relates to her as a person or

to her occupational role as a psychologist. As shown below, she is very clear in the matter.]

Lata: As a person, not as a psychologist because I'm very sure that my sessions would bring about a change in the client.

Windy: OK. So, you seem to be saying that, 'If I tell them openly what my fee is – it's 1500 rupees – and they say, 'No, I'm not going to pay it,' or they say, 'Yes,' and they try to negotiate downwards and then you say, 'No, it's 1500 rupees,' and then they say, 'Thank you, but I'm not coming back,'' you would judge yourself as inadequate as a person? Is that what you're saying?

Lata: … Yeah, or maybe I'm not helping the other person enough. I should understand from what space they're coming.

Windy: So, sorry, you need to understand what space they're coming from?

Lata: … Probably, yes.

Windy: I don't understand what that means. I don't understand what you mean by what space they're coming from.

Lata: So, it's more like why are they trying to negotiate the fee downwards, because probably they wouldn't have done that with any doctor or any other professional.

Windy: Perhaps you're right. Perhaps they're more likely to think that, because psychologists are open to negotiation and doctors aren't, that they'll try to negotiate with a psychologist. But that doesn't explain, because most psychologists would probably say, 'No,' you see.

Lata: Right.

Windy: But this particular psychologist is reluctant. Let me put it the other way round: for you to feel adequate as a person, what would they have to do? How would they show you certain things that you would then say, 'Ah, wait a minute, I am now adequate as a person'?

Lata: In that case, I think more than them, I should be able to tell them that, 'This is my fee.'

Windy: No, that's the goal. I'm not asking you about the goal. I'm asking you about the problem.

Lata: OK.

Windy: Right?

Lata: Yeah.

Windy: So, what I'm saying is, if certain conditions existed and then you'd say, 'Oh, wait a minute, I'm now adequate as a person,' it sounds like to me first of all that, for you to be adequate as a person, you would tell them your fee and they would accept it and that you would tell them your fee and they wouldn't negotiate and they would think they're getting value for money.

Lata: Yeah. So, I'm fine if they asked me, 'OK, what is the fee?' and then said, 'Is there a package kind of a thing that you offer, like five sessions or 10 sessions.'

Windy: Let's not go there. Let's just stick with what we've got which is the one session – they're trying to negotiate a deal and you want to say no. What I'm saying is, if you judged yourself as adequate, would you say no?

[As can be seen, I am having a little trouble clarifying the nature of the problem and keeping Lata focused. My hypothesis is that this is a problem resulting from a philosophy of conditional self-worth and I have been trying to clarify what conditions have to exist for her to be adequate.]

Lata: Yes, I would judge myself as adequate if I was open about the possibility to say no to them, if it was possible.

Windy: Yeah. So, it sounds like your adequacy is in your hands or in their hands?

Lata: In my hands.

Windy: No, I mean in terms of the problem.

Lata: In terms of the problem, I feel it's in their hands.

Windy: Right, OK. So, as a psychologist, is that a good place to place your adequacy?

Lata: No.

Windy: No. Where's the best place to place your adequacy?

Lata: It should be with me.

Windy: Ideally. Right.

Lata: Yes.

[*Lata seems to see that from the perspective of her problem she has placed her adequacy as a person in the hands of her clients where in reality it is in her hands.*]

Windy: OK. You see, what we have in REBT is we might call it 'unconditional adequacy', alright, which is, 'I'm going to regard myself as adequate as a person and tell them my fee whether or not they accept it or whether or not they negotiate.' Now, wouldn't that solve your problem?

Lata: Yes, it would.

Windy: You sound hesitant.

Lata: Yes. So, again, the same thought comes: would they come for the session or not?

Windy: But, again, you're judging your adequacy on the basis of whether they come or not, right?

Lata: Right. Right.

Windy: Because, if you said, 'I'm going to regard myself as adequate as a person whether they accept my fee, whether or not they try to negotiate and whether they come back or not.'

Lata: Yeah.

Windy: 'I'm still adequate.'

Lata: Right, yes.

Windy: Now, if you believed that, wouldn't that solve your problem?

Lata: Yes, it would.

[After some hesitancy, Lata seems to grasp that the solution to her problem is unconditional self-adequacy, which is in her hands.]

Windy: OK. So, listen, let's suppose you were supervising – how long have you been in the field for?

Lata: I have been exclusively in this field for the past 10 years.

Windy: Ten years. And do you supervise any junior psychologist?

Lata: Yes, I have.

Windy: You do. Now, let's suppose a junior psychologist came to you and you said, 'Now, listen, before we start, let's get a few things straight: your adequacy as a person is dependent upon whether or not your clients accept your fee, whether or not they negotiate or whether or not they come back,' right? 'If they come back, if they accept your fee and if they don't try and negotiate, you're adequate as a person and, if they quibble or if they refuse to take your fee and if they don't come back, you are inadequate as a person,' would you teach your supervisee that?

Lata: No, I wouldn't.

Windy: Why not? Why wouldn't you teach your supervisee that?

Lata: Because the client does not determine their adequacy or inadequacy.

[*This is a tailored version of the friend dispute, where the therapist asks the client whether they would teach a friend the same rigid/extreme attitudes that they hold themselves.*]

Windy: OK. So, let me get this straight: their clients don't determine their adequacy but your clients determine your adequacy?

[*This is an important part of the friend dispute – to create a state of cognitive dissonance that the person needs to resolve.*]

Lata: No, they don't.

Windy: Well, fine, but you've got to act accordingly, right?

[*Note that immediately I introduce the idea of acting in ways that are consistent with the new idea of unconditional self-adequacy.*]

Lata: Right.

Windy: When's the next time you have the opportunity to tell people what your fee is?

[*To capitalise on the work we have done, I ask Lata to identify a scenario where she can implement to attitudinal solution.*]

Lata: Tomorrow morning.

Windy: OK. So, let's imagine tomorrow morning comes and you're preparing this: you say, 'Now, wait a minute, part of me believes that my adequacy is going to be dependent upon how they respond to that and part of me doesn't. Which part do I want to strengthen and which part do I want to weaken?' Now, what's your answer to that?

Lata: So, I would want to strengthen my part that I'm adequate irrespective of what the client says and weaken the part where I think that the client has a say in my adequacy or inadequacy.

Windy: Yes, and are you prepared to do that uncomfortably?

Lata: Yes.

Windy: Because you're not going to be comfortable doing that until you do it a number of times.

[I emphasize the likelihood that Lata will be uncomfortable implementing the solution but that a) that does not need to stop her doing so and b) doing so with repetition will help her to become more comfortable.]

Lata: Right.

Windy: OK?

Lata: Yes.

Windy: OK. So, let's do a little roleplay. I'll be a client, right?

[Here I am suggesting that Lata rehearses the solution that we developed.]

Lata: OK.

Windy: OK. And I want you to see how you hold to it. Now, in this conversation, get into the frame of mind that your adequacy as a person is not dependent upon my response to anything, OK?

Lata: Right.

Windy: OK. So, I ring you up: 'OK, oh, Lata, I'd like to come and see you for counselling.'

Lata: 'OK. That's fine. So, when should we schedule the counselling for?'

Windy: 'When are you free?'

Lata: 'I am free on Thursday at 2pm.'

Windy: 'That's a good time for me.'

Lata: 'Alright. So, I would like to tell you that my fee is rupees 1500 per session.'

Windy: '1500?'

Lata: 'Yes, it is 1500.'

Windy: 'That's a lot of money.'

Lata: 'But that's what I charge and that's my charges.'

Windy: 'Can't you reduce it?'

Lata: 'No, not as of now.'

Windy: 'OK, thank you very much but I think that's too expensive for me. I think I'm going to go and find somebody else. Is that OK?'

Lata: 'Yes, absolutely fine. It's no problem.'

Windy: 'OK, bye-bye.'

Lata: 'Bye, all the best.'

Windy: 'Bye.' Right, how do you feel?

Lata: I felt much more looser than before, otherwise I would get tightened up.

Windy: And how come you felt looser? What was the change in your thinking that helped you to become looser?

[Whenever someone reports a change then it is important that I help myself and them identify how they brought about such change.]

Lata: Yeah, because I thought that it is me who decides and not the other person who would decide.

Windy: That's right. OK. So, would you like to do that every time you have a new client?

Lata: Yes.

Windy: Right. Because, in doing that, you'll get more comfortable, you'll strengthen the belief and the clients, some you're going to lose and some you're not going to lose.

Lata: Right.

Windy: Right? Is there anything about this problem that we haven't touched on yet?

Lata: No. No, we have touched everything, because I was not able to bring that shift in my thought.

Windy: Right. And now you are?

Lata: Yes, now I am. To be honest, it wasn't easy, but now I feel confident that I can.

Windy: Good. And don't forget, a shift in thinking reinforces a shift in behaviour and a shift in behaviour reinforces a shift in thinking. They go together.

Lata: Yes.

Windy: OK?

Lata: Yes.

Windy: Good. By the way, if you want a copy of the transcript and the recording, just write to me at my email address: windy@windydryden.com. It's very simple.

Lata: OK. I shall be writing to you.

Windy: Yeah, OK. Lovely, OK. So, let's see what the group think.

4

Helping the Person to Address Her Anxiety about Practising Socratic Questioning in Therapy

Windy–A.M. Devlin: Interview on 22/02/21
Length: 17 minutes 14 secs

Windy: Hi, A.M. Devlin, how are you today?

A.M. Devlin: Hello. Yes, I'm very well, thank you very much. And yourself?

Windy: Yes, not too bad. Now, what is your understanding of the purpose of our conversation today?

A.M. Devlin: I understand it to be if anyone with a type of problem that they have within maybe the therapy room or within themselves that they could ask a question to see if there are any solutions or practice, any types of methods to overcome it or get better at it.

Windy: And what problem or issue are you looking for help today?

A.M. Devlin: Well, for myself, I graduated in October '19 and I've not had much interaction with clients. I feel confident in myself – last week you said can we talk the talk or walk the walk, and I believe walk the talk, which was very good, and I believe I can walk the talk. But, when it comes to it, it's my ability to use Socratic questioning. I feel I get very nervous and anxious and then my mind just goes blank.

Windy: So, you're anxious about using Socratic questioning in counselling?

A.M. Devlin: Yes.

Windy: Right, OK. Have you ever had the experience of becoming nervous about doing anything like that before and then, having had the opportunity or the experience of overcoming it?

A.M. Devlin: I worked in the probation office and I delivered programmes for prisoners, intervention programmes, and we used to have a psychologist, but it was more about the prisoners than ourselves, to offload.

Windy: Yeah, but were you nervous about using any interventions there?

A.M. Devlin: Yes.

Windy: And how did you deal with your nerves or your anxiety?

A.M. Devlin: Well, what I did was I used to, obviously, go along to the programme, deliver the programme as best as I could and then I would just sit and actually do a wee bit of self-reflection myself on where I think I went wrong or how I could've done better.

Windy: And what kind of reflection was that? Was that
                    a helpful reflection or was that an unhelpful
                    reflection?

A.M. Devlin: It was probably a bit unhelpful, because I'm
                    quite hard on myself, then. I began to get a
                    little bit better by easing off on myself, by
                    saying, 'You must've done something or doing
                    something right to get where you are just
                    now.' So, that's what I hold onto.

Windy: And, so, did you learn through that process or
                    a process like that not to be nervous about the
                    interventions that you were delivering to the
                    prisoners?

A.M. Devlin: Not so much then, but, taking myself through
                    the course for my diploma that I did for two
                    years, I learnt a lot more personally. So, that's
                    why I'm not as hard on myself now.

Windy: OK. So, what would happen if you brought
                    your attitude that's not hard on yourself to
                    Socratic questioning? What would that sound
                    like?

*[What I have done here is to help A.M. Devlin identify a
situation where she addressed her nervousness about doing
something and encouraging her to see that she can do
something similar about dealing with her anxiety about using
Socratic questioning in counselling.]*

A.M. Devlin: I think it would be..., I'm quite good at
                    understanding what the problem is with the
                    client and I've got... good listening skills.

Windy: So, 'I can understand what the client's talking about, I've got good listening skills,' yeah. What else?

A.M. Devlin: … I'm very empathetic and sometimes a bit similar maybe to a situation, I can be kind of sympathetic but not to the degree that it's on a personal level.

Windy: OK. So, you've got a lot of skills that you can actually bring to the reflections before and afterwards, OK?

A.M. Devlin: Yeah.

Windy: Now, let's see if we can zero in on what you're particularly anxious about vis-à-vis the Socratic questioning. What would you say that you were most anxious about when it comes to using Socratic questioning in counselling?

A.M. Devlin: It's just sometimes the who, the what, the when, all these kinds of things. When I start to use that depending on where we are in the session, I feel like I'm repeating myself.

Windy: Well, yes, you may be repeating yourself. That's quite correct. You may or you may not. But what are you anxious about?

A.M. Devlin: I think I'm just anxious that I believe that I'm not good enough, probably, a core belief creeping in at the end of the day, probably.

Windy: Yeah, but before we get to the core belief, are you saying that, 'I'm not good enough at the moment to do the Socratic questioning'?

A.M. Devlin: Yes. I'm not good enough. A part of me says 'at the moment' and then a part of me says 'it's never going to be', but I think that's got a lot to do with the COVID situation, maybe.

Windy: Well, because it sounds like you're saying, 1) 'I would like to be good at Socratic questioning,' – is that right?

[While A.M. Devlin mentions 'core beliefs' and never statements, my focus is on helping her identify the rigid attitude that underpins her anxiety. I do this initially by taking her preference as listed above.]

A.M. Devlin: Yes, very much so.

Windy: And when would you like to be good at Socratic questioning?

A.M. Devlin: Well, even in just general conversation with different people.

Windy: No, but I'm talking about in therapy. You're seeing somebody and you're anxious when you're using it and you're saying part of you is saying, 'I want to be good at Socratic questioning,' and I'm asking you when?

A.M. Devlin: From the start.

[I often find it important to discover a person's time frame when discussing their anxiety issue as shown below I incorporate this into their preference.]

Windy: Right, OK. That's fine, because it would be nice if you were skilful at the start. That would be nice. It's unlikely, but it would be nice if that happened. But, when you're anxious, do you think you're saying, 'I'd like to be good at Socratic questioning at the start, but I don't have to be. I can record it and learn it and bring my self-reflective skills,' or do you think you're really saying, 'I want to be good at Socratic questioning at the start and, therefore, I must be good at Socratic questioning at the start'?

[*This is a common intervention that I use. I take the person's preference and ask them to say that when they are anxious whether they are making this preference rigid or keeping it flexible.*]

A.M. Devlin: Yeah, the second one. Yeah.

Windy: OK. Now, can you see then the relationship between that demand and your anxiety?

A.M. Devlin: Yes.

Windy: Right. So, what would be your goal?

A.M. Devlin: So, I could then take that demand away from using Socratic questioning.

Windy: And what would that sound like, do you think?

A.M. Devlin: … Well, it's just relax, don't put so much pressure on yourself that your mind's going to go blank. Just see what happens.

Windy: Well, right, but that's a little vague.

A.M. Devlin: Right, OK.

Windy: Because, if you really were more focused on your desire, you'd say, 'I'd like to be good straight away at Socratic questioning, but I don't have to be.' Now, if you really believed that, how would you feel about making mistakes about Socratic questioning, if you were wanting but not demanding that you'd be able to be good at this straight away?

[*Because A.M. Devlin is struggling to clearly articulate her flexible attitude, I do this for her and then ask about the emotional consequence of having conviction in this attitude.*]

A.M. Devlin: I'd probably feel less anxious. I would still have a little bit of anxiety.

Windy: Well, I'd say you'd feel concerned, because you still would want to do it well straight from the start. But, if you really were convinced that you didn't have to, then you'd actually be concerned. We'd want you to be concerned because the concern would motivate you to learn from your mistakes, wouldn't it?

[*Here, I help A.M. Devlin to distinguish between anxiety (an unhealthy negative emotion in REBT) and concern (a healthy negative emotion.*]

A.M. Devlin: Yeah, absolutely.

Windy: But then what you said earlier is that you start off by saying, 'I'm not good enough at the moment at Socratic questioning,' right?

A.M. Devlin: OK.

Windy: And you might not be, and the way to become good enough at it is to do what?

A.M. Devlin: … Practise, to learn more.

Windy: Practise it, record it, go over it. That's what I do with my single-session therapy sessions. I record it, I read it, I say, 'That was stupid,' and I learn from that. I actually say, 'That's stupid, but I'm not a stupid person,' you see?

A.M. Devlin: Yeah.

Windy: But the other thing you're saying is, 'I'm not good enough at the moment and, therefore, I'm not good enough, full stop,' right? Now, how does that follow that, if you're not good enough at Socratic questioning at any given time, that that proves that you, A.M. Devlin, are not good enough as a person, full stop?

A.M. Devlin: ... [*pause*] Yeah, so that would probably just be my own beliefs about different...

Windy: Yeah. I'm saying how does it follow?

A.M. Devlin: How does it follow to?

Windy: How does it follow that, if you're not good enough at Socratic questioning at any given time, that that is proof that you are not good enough as a person, full stop?

[*Here, I help A.M. Devlin to focus and examine her self-devaluation attitude that because she is not good at Socratic questioning this proves she is not good as a person.*]

A.M. Devlin: Right, aha. Well,... because I could sit back and say that to myself, which I do, but, if I then went out and did something about that and practised what you said, that would then lessen the belief that I'm not good enough at

Socratic questioning now or I'll never be. Well, how will I know that?

Windy: Right, yeah, exactly, because you create the never by demanding that you have to be good at it now.

[*Here I show A.M. Devlin that a rigid attitude serves to create never thinking.*]

A.M. Devlin: Yes.

Windy: But let's just stick to my questioning. Would you teach a client that, if they were not good enough at something, that that is proof that they were not good enough as a person, full stop? Would you teach that to the client?

[*This question serves to encourage the client to view a self-devaluation attitude from a different perspective.*]

A.M. Devlin: No way.

Windy: Why not?

A.M. Devlin: Well, that's just reinforcing their belief.

Windy: Yeah, but why wouldn't you want to teach them that?

A.M. Devlin: Because we want to learn new skills to increase our ability to change.

Windy: That's right and, if you reinforce their idea that they're not good enough, they're not going to have a very easy time at teaching themselves new skills, are they?

A.M. Devlin: That's right.

Windy: So, you're clear that you wouldn't teach them that?

A.M. Devlin: Oh no. No.

Windy: So, why would you continue to teach yourself that?

A.M. Devlin: Well, like that, that's quite refreshing, yes.

[It is clear that this change of perspective has had an impact on A.M. Devlin.]

Windy: Right. That's right. And the answer is you have a choice: you can either continue to teach yourself that or you could start teaching yourself something different. Now, what attitude towards yourself could you start teaching you, A.M. Devlin, to actually become concerned rather than anxious about learning any new skill as you go forward? What attitude could you teach yourself about you?

A.M. Devlin: Well, if I don't make mistakes, I'm not going to learn from them.

Windy: 'And, if I do make mistakes...'

A.M. Devlin: And, if I do make mistakes, then I'm not going to give myself a hard time about it. It's just something that I need to learn.

Windy: But, if you were to put that into something more concrete, what does 'I'm not going to give myself a hard time'? What does that sound like when you spell out the attitude?

[A.M. Devlin is a little vague in her responses and thus I help her to see what more concrete responses would be like.]

A.M. Devlin: … I am not going to give myself a hard time as I am worth doing this.

Windy: Yeah. 'I'm worth doing it because I'm human, alive, fallible and unique. My acceptance of myself is going to be dependent upon those things. So, if I ever become infallible, if I ever become simple, if I ever become unhuman, then I could put myself down. But, as I continue to be human, I'm going to have a choice to accept myself or reject myself, and I'm going to choose to accept myself even though I may have rejected myself in the past.'

A.M. Devlin: … Reject.

Windy: Yeah.

A.M. Devlin: Yeah.

Windy: And, if you practised that going forward, you sit down and say, 'Right, today in this counselling session I'm going to use Socratic questioning. I want to master it straight away, but I don't have to and, if I don't, it proves I'm a fallible human being. It doesn't prove I'm not good enough,' if you really practised that philosophy, what do you think would happen when you brought yourself to the Socratic questioning?

[Here I am introducing a future scenario to help A.M. Devlin rehearse her attitudinal solution to see what difference it would make to how she feels about doing Socratic questioning.]

A.M. Devlin: I think it would come much more naturally, because the pressure's away, I'm believing in myself. I think they're just going to start to come out and then I'll probably find more confidence, because then I'll see that the clients are opening up more because I'm asking the right questions.

Windy: Right, but you still might make mistakes.

A.M. Devlin: Yeah.

Windy: Yeah, do you know why?

A.M. Devlin: Yes, just because I don't know it.

Windy: That's right, and Socratic questioning is not an easy skill to master, you see?

A.M. Devlin: Yeah, absolutely. Yeah, because I've got some examples of Socratic questioning.

Windy: Yeah. But, when you calm down and you practise that healthy philosophy, you could go on YouTube, there are YouTube videos of Socratic questionings and things like that, but, at the moment, if you look at those YouTube videos, you'll be bringing your anxious self to the viewing and that's not going to help you in any shape or form.

A.M. Devlin: Yeah.

Windy: Alright, so, why don't you summarise the work we've done today, A.M. Devlin.

A.M. Devlin: OK. So, basically, what I'm going to try to do is have more acceptance of myself being a human and I do have a choice: I can either reject myself or accept myself, and practise more by doing recordings, doing more self-reflections, believe that I'm a human being and I'm valuable, and about having that healthy psychology kind of thinking. Then I should possibly then be more relaxed and don't take [unclear] with me.

[I often ask people to summarise the work I have done with them in the conversation. A.M. Devlin's response shows that she resonated more with the unconditional self-acceptance attitude than with the flexible attitude as a way of dealing with her anxiety.]

Windy: And then you could bring this attitude and you could generalise it to when you learn any new skill, not only in counselling and psychotherapy, but any new skill afterwards. That's what you can do.

[Here, I make the point that she can generalise this learning to learning any new skill.]

A.M. Devlin: Yeah.

Windy: Now, have I helped you to your satisfaction today?

A.M. Devlin: You certainly have, Mr Dryden, you certainly have. Thank you very much.

Windy: Good. OK, let's get the group's questions.

5

Helping the Person to Take the Horror Out of Tragedy

Windy – Daniele: Interview on 22/03/21
Length: 11 minutes 46 secs

Windy: Hi Daniele, what's your understanding of the purpose of our conversation today?

Daniele: Hi Windy.

Windy: Hi.

Daniele: Well, you're helping me resolve a problem.

Windy: That's the theory. What problem would you like to be helped with?

Daniele: OK, well, I have anxiety. I work at a high school and right now, with COVID, everyone's still with online mode. So, it's been hard on the kids. A lot of them are struggling with depression. So, we're seeing a lot of them, but, unfortunately, a lot of people don't come in for counselling. So, I guess the anxiety I have is about one of the kids taking their own life.

Windy: One of the kids that you've been seeing or one of the kids you haven't been seeing?

Daniele: I think just in the school.

Windy: Well, OK, let's suppose that that tragedy happens. That's a tragedy because children do take their own lives and that would be a tragedy. You'd better be what I call healthily concerned about that possibility rather than unhealthily anxious about that. Do you know why?

[*Right from the outset, I outline that concern about this tragedy is the healthy alternative to anxiety about tragedy and then ask the person why this is the case. Albert Ellis used to employ this strategy in his demonstrations a lot. He would assert the REBT position and then ask the volunteer to provide reasons to support the position.*]

Daniele: ... Well, if I'm healthily concerned about it, then I'll be able to mobilise and maybe even do some prevention.

[*This strategy pays off immediately. Daniele can see that concern will help her to face and process the adversity and that (see below) anxiety will have the opposite effect.*]

Windy: That's right, whereas anxiety is disturbance and how does you being disturbed help you think in a creative way about how to save the lives of people who are also feeling disturbed?

Daniele: It does the opposite.

Windy: That's right.

Daniele: It makes me avoid it. It makes me turn off.

Windy: Right. So, what do you think you're mainly anxious about in terms of your attitude? You're saying, 'One of our school kids may take their own lives and that would be,' what?

[*Here I outline the AC elements of Daniele's problem and use the sentence completion technique so that she can provide her B.*]

Daniele: That'll be awful. That will be the worst thing. That will be terrible.

Windy: Now, you see, you're not distinguishing between tragic and awful. Your choice is between tragic plus awful or tragic minus awful. What choice do you want to take?

[*Daniele's basic attitude at B is 'awfulising'. In this response I help her to see what that she has a choice between her awfulising attitude ('tragedy plus awful') and a non-awfulising attitude alternative ('tragedy minus awful').*]

Daniele: … Well, I don't know. … [Pause] It is awful.

Windy: No, it's not awful. You keep hanging onto this idea that it's awful. I'm saying it's tragic. Awful means that you can't transcend it. There's no possibility of going forward in life. It's the end of things. It says awful is the end of the world, that's it, finished, we pack up and go home. Tragedy without awful means it is tragic and nothing I would ever say to take away the tragedy, but that, after a period of mourning, people will regroup and move on, as would you.

[*As Daniele is confused, I respond by outlining the meaning of both 'tragedy plus awful' and 'tragedy minus awful' so that she can more clearly discriminate between the two.*]

Daniele: Yes.

Windy: So, your job is to take the horror out of tragedy, not the tragedy out of tragedy.

[*I could have phrased this as a question: 'So is your job to take the horror out of tragedy or to keep the horror in?'. This would have engaged her better.*]

Daniele: Yes, I agree with that.

Windy: Yeah. So, how can you do that?

Daniele: … [*pause*] Maybe make some statements about… the coping: that life does go on even though this is a horrible situation; that this is a tragic situation.

[*In these situations, the language that Daniele uses with herself is important. Note that she does not discriminate between 'a horrible situation' and a 'tragic situation'. I still have to help her to make this discrimination more keenly.*]

Windy: A tragic situation, yeah. And, incidentally, if you really emphasise the tragedy, which is what it is, and recognise that, every time you're adding words when you're anxious like 'terrible' and 'awful', you're really taking a tragedy and you're adding horror to it and that doesn't help the person who's died, it doesn't help you, it doesn't help their loved ones. In fact, it gets in the way. Now, the thing to do is to ask yourself this: when you're anxious about this as a possibility, how does that affect your behaviour? What do you do when you're anxious?

Daniele: … [*Pause*] Well, it's not really a behaviour, but I avoid thinking about it.

Windy: OK. And what would you do if you were concerned but not anxious about this tragedy? What would you think about it?

Daniele: I would, I guess in the back of my mind, 1) prepare for the emergency situation if it were to happen and, 2) I guess think about what else I can do in terms of prevention.

Windy: Right, and recognise that your job is to do all you can humanly do, but that isn't going to necessarily mean that people aren't going to kill themselves. I have had three suicides of clients who I was actively seeing and they're difficult to deal with and I really had to accept the fact that I was doing all I could, but unfortunately it wasn't enough. It's not a nice feeling, but I'm not anxious. I didn't give up the profession or anything like that. So, if you recognise that all you can do is do what you can do humanly and that doesn't mean that tragic things aren't going to happen, and then you think about it, because part of your problem is that you don't think about it and, therefore, not thinking about it, you maintain it. But, if you think about it, really sit down and say to yourself, 'Now, look, Daniele, it would be really tragic but it wouldn't be terrible and, in taking that, I'm not being insensitive because I'm sensitive to the tragedy, but I don't want to add my disturbance to it, because it adds nothing to it and it only stops me from managing my issues and thinking about it and coming up with a plan, but, when I come up with a plan, I do have to accept there's no guarantee that, if I come up with a plan, it's going to prevent the tragedy from happening.'

[*Here, I use self-disclosure to show how I responded healthily to occasions in my career when my clients tragically committed suicide. Also, note that I make the point that adopting a non-awfulising attitude does not mean that Daniele is being insensitive to the tragedy. She has not made reference to this, but as it a common objection to a person adopting a non-awfulising attitude I do so myself.*]

Daniele: … Yeah, I guess I could just make myself sit down and formulate a plan, write down a plan of the go-to.

Windy: That's right and, even if you're concerned about the tragedy, you'd still be uncomfortable with it because it is an uncomfortable situation to think about, but, as you say, if you do that and you bear the discomfort and you show yourself that there's a good reason to bear the discomfort because you can really go through and process. You see, you're not processing. You're stuck, because you're saying, 'Oh my God, it's terrible. Stop thinking,' right?

[*Here I introduce the idea of the importance of bearing the discomfort of acknowledging that the tragedy could happen and formulating a plan to deal with.*]

Daniele: Yes.

Windy: And therefore you don't process. You don't put it into its healthy perspective, you don't come up with a plan, you stop thinking and that will just maintain the problem. So, why don't you summarise where we've got to today?

[*Here, I make the point that by holding an awfulising attitude Daniele does not make a constructive plan to deal with the tragedy of a student killing themself if this happens. Her thinking avoidance maintains her anxiety problem. Then, as is common in my very brief single session work, I ask the client to summarise the work we have done together.*]

Daniele: OK. So, stop telling myself that it is awful because, even though it is a tragedy, life does go on. And to then think about my ability to bear it and also to formulate a plan so I can process it instead of the usual avoidance.

Windy: Right. Now, let me teach you what I call the surgeon technique. Do you want to hear the surgeon technique?

Daniele: Love it.

Windy: OK. So, imagine that you have an illness and you have to have a complicated operation, but you've got very good private health insurance, so you get to choose your surgeon. Now, it's top of the range insurance, so they give you a choice of surgeons and they're all equally skilful, but they have a different attitude. So, which surgeon would you choose on the basis of their attitude given the fact they're equally skilful? Surgeon 1 comes in and says, 'OK, I guarantee that nothing will go wrong. I'm completely and utterly convinced that this will go well and I'm so convinced that at some point during the operation I might close my eyes, but don't worry, nothing will go wrong.' That's Surgeon 1. Surgeon 2 comes in and says, 'Oh my God, you could die. That would be awful. That would be awful. Oh my God. I couldn't bear it. I can't think about it. It's terrible.' Surgeon 3 comes in and says, 'Look, this is a complicated situation. You could die. That would be a tragedy, but I'm not turning that into a horror. I'm going to do all the best I can and I'm going to concentrate because I'm not turning a tragedy into a horror.' Which surgeon would you choose to do the operation?

Daniele: The last one.

Windy: Why?

Daniele: Because Surgeon 1 is giving me BS and Surgeon 2
               is just the whacko.

Windy: Yeah. So, which counsellor are you? A BS
               counsellor, a whacko counsellor or a realistic
               counsellor?

Daniele: Well, I want to be the realistic counsellor.

Windy: Then take the horror out of tragedy, as Surgeon 3
               did. Surgeon 3 can do his job because he has taken
               the horror out of tragedy. Surgeon 2 kept the
               horror with tragedy and you described him rightly
               as a whacko. So, bear that in mind that every time
               you add horror to the tragedy of somebody taking
               their own life, you're turning yourself into a
               whacko counsellor.

*[The 'surgeon technique' helps Daniele to choose what she
calls the 'realistic surgeon'. I find that this technique is a
useful aid to helping people take the horror out of adversity.]*

Daniele: Yeah. So, what I've been doing is the Surgeon 1
               and 2 talking to each other.

Windy: Yeah, that's right.

Daniele: 'This is horrible.' 'No, everything's going to be
               OK.'

*[This is a very important point, and I am pleased that Daniele
comes up with it herself. She alternates between what I call
'threat-related thinking' and 'safety-seeking thinking (Dryden,
2022) and in doing so, she maintains her anxiety problem
because she does not take the horror out of tragedy and*

engage in the realistic thinking that a non-awfulising attitude will help her to access.]

Windy: 'No, it won't happen.' 'It's horrible.' 'It won't happen.' 'It's horrible.' 'It won't happen.' Right, and look where it's got you.

Daniele: Yeah, anxious.

Windy: Yeah, exactly. If you want to be anxious, just keep those two talking to each other. If you want to be healthily concerned but not anxious, engage with the realistic surgeon and the realistic counsellor attitude. OK, let's get their reflections. Thank you very much.

6

Helping the Person to Develop a Flexible Attitude Towards Not Living Up to Her Ideal

Windy–Emily: Interview on 20/10/20
Length: 19 minutes 45 secs

Windy: What is your understanding of the purpose of our conversation this evening?

Emily: So, my understanding is that, with a problem that I have, that you can help talk me through it to unpick where my rational and irrational thoughts are perhaps preventing me from moving on and being able to either live with the problem in a comfortable way or perhaps even eradicate it.

Windy: So, in terms of what you have just said, do I take it that you have had prior exposure to rational emotive behaviour therapy?

[*As I explained at the beginning of the book, the transcripts that appear in this book are of sessions that I do for the REBT Facebook Group and, as such, many people who watch and volunteer for these sessions are knowledgeable about REBT or, like Emily, are REB therapists or trainees.*]

Emily: So, I'm embarking on my own training. So, I've been doing quite a bit of background reading and starting to understand the concepts. So, this opportunity came about which seemed like an ideal situation for me to learn more about REBT but also start to apply it to things that are going on in my life.

Windy: OK. So, in terms of the particular problem that you'd like to focus on today, can I just ask you before we start have you tried to utilise REBT on this particular problem that we're going to be discussing?

[Given that Emily is training to be an REB therapist, I ask her if she has used REBT to help herself with her problem. Asking people how they have tried to solve their problem in the past is a common question in single-session work.]

Emily: No, I haven't because I'm struggling to understand it. I'm struggling to be able to make those connections of understanding why my brain and my actions are linked and I can't quite get there.

Windy: OK. Well, let's see if I can help you to get there. So, could you tell me, as specifically as you can, what problem that you would like me to help you with this evening?

Emily: So, from the age of 16 I was in a relationship for 16 years that was quite toxic and manipulative. And I had lots of dreams and ambitions and I felt at that time, particularly when I was in my 20s, that I really knew what it was that I wanted to do, but I wasn't allowed. I had two young children and my husband at the time was very restrictive on what it was that was going to be acceptable to the family.

I left that relationship after 16 years and I'm now on the path to doing what it is that I want to do and trying to restart those dreams and those ambitions, but I have a habit of not quite believing that they're possible and I'll get to a certain point and I'll run away from it and I'll stop. I won't necessarily complete what it is that I set out to do. And I think that I have quite a lot of resentment and anger surrounding the fact that I didn't do it when I was in my 20s and I feel like I'm kind of 15, 20 years behind the curve.

Windy: Right. And, so, you would like to refocus on what your dreams are?

Emily: Yeah.

Windy: And yet you're aware of two things: one is that you have a tendency to run away from it and, also, secondly, that you have a sense of resentment for all those years wasted?

Emily: Yeah, very much so.

Windy: Which obstacle do you think, if we helped you with tonight, would lead you to take a significant step forward?

[*As can be seen, Emily's problem has a number of elements, and, as is typical of brief single-session work, it is important that I help her focus on one of these elements in the session that we are having.*]

Emily: I think the resentment issue because I think that it's the underlying problem that keeps cropping up and I don't particularly want to carry on for the rest of my life feeling that anger, that frustration, that resentment over what should have been. I want to lay that to rest, really.

Windy: So, who or what are you resentful towards?

Emily: I think I'm resentful towards myself mostly. I'm cross that I chose to spend as much time as I did with somebody who was holding me back and I'm angry with myself for not – I feel I see it that I didn't have the strength to push forward and to stand my ground enough on the things that I really wanted to do and that I was too interested in making sure that I was doing the things he wanted me to do.

Windy: Do you think you didn't have the strength or you didn't use the strength that you had?

Emily: I don't feel I used it,… really, yeah. I don't think that I used it. I think it was there all the time, but it got squashed.

Windy: Right. And, so, you're feeling resentful towards yourself for not doing what?

Emily: Probably for standing up to him and finding a way. I'm quite a resourceful person and I am determined, but it's quite tricky… to put into words, really.

Windy: So, looking back, how do you think you stopped yourself from standing up to him and perhaps being able to put yourself into a situation where you could've pursued your dreams earlier? How do you think you stopped yourself?

[*Although Emily's stated focus is on her self-resentment, my aim here is to find out a little about why Emily did not stand up to her ex-husband so I can use this to help her to deal effectively with her resentment towards herself.*]

Emily: I used other people as an excuse and I put other people's needs first.

Windy: But, as it was an excuse, it seems to hide the real reason.

Emily: Yeah. … Yeah, that's true. … [Pause] Yeah. That's an interesting one.

Windy: OK. Would you like to just reflect on that for a moment?

Emily: Yeah, I think so. … [Pause] I think there was probably quite a lot of doubt. Whilst I can have dreams, I don't necessarily truly believe that I'm able to achieve them. It's almost like it can't be possible for me.

[*As the conversation unfolds, Emily realises that she has not pursued her dreams because she has doubted that she could achieve them*]

Windy: So, you have dreams but you really doubt whether you can really have the wherewithal to bring about those dreams.

Emily: Yeah.

Windy: And it sounds like it served a purpose for you to put the emphasis on others: 'Oh, I couldn't do this because of this person,' rather than to come face to face with that part of yourself that was really, really doubtful.

Emily: Yes, I think that you're right. I was able to use the responsibilities that I had of, say for example bringing up my children and being a wife there for me. Yeah, it probably was, actually. Yeah, just a way of me avoiding confronting what was really going on.

Windy: What relationship do you have now with that part of Emily that is doubtful and that she can pursue her dreams? Looking back, what relationship do you have with her?

Emily: I'm still fighting with her a lot. I'm fighting and I have won some battles because I am taking steps towards achieving those dreams, but the doubtful Emily is still singing quite loudly.

Windy: You say you have children, is that correct?

Emily: Yeah.

Windy: Could you tell me a little bit about your children?

[*What is in my mind here is to use a technique that I call 'Teach Your Children Well' whereby I say to the person how would they respond to one their children who has their same problem. I do this to promote a state of cognitive dissonance where the person is in conflict between treating their children in one way and treating themselves in the opposite way.*]

Emily: Yeah, I've got two girls: one who's 15 who's living in a different part of the country with her dad at the moment; and then I've got one with me as well.

Windy: Are they confident or are they also doubtful about their own capabilities?

Emily: The elder one is very doubtful and the younger one is very confident but probably has an underlying doubt about her. She's very ambitious.

Windy: And have you found that the best therapeutic way of dealing with your kids' doubts about themselves is to fight with them about it?

Emily: No.

Windy: You haven't?

Emily: No, I don't at all.

Windy: Why not?

Emily: Because that would get you nowhere.

Windy: I'm sorry, I'm getting a bit hard of hearing these days. What did you just say?

[*The 'hard of hearing' technique encourages the person to state something healthy with greater emphasis.*]

Emily: That would get you nowhere.

Windy: That would get you nowhere, OK.

Emily: Yeah.

Windy: OK. So, let me just ask you to stand back and reflect on what you just said.

Emily: Yes. Yeah. I should. Yeah, no, agreed.

Windy: So, if your kids are doubtful, how do you approach them?

Emily: I try to get them to focus on their strengths and how far they have come and how it's always building blocks: life is part of creating building blocks so that you can move on to other things.

Windy: Right. So, it sounds like, if you were to follow your own advice towards yourself right now, I think it sounds to me that you've got a choice: one is to actually utilise the same approach towards yourself which would be an encouraging one, to focus on your strengths, maybe also to be compassionate towards that Emily who was scared to stand up for herself and to go forward and actually hid behind her own doubts, to be compassionate, or you could fight with that person and be resentful towards her. I don't know which one you think you'd like to do.

Emily: I think I might prefer Option 1, to be honest. Yeah.

Windy: Right. So, when you've chosen Option 2 and you're fighting with yourself and being resentful, what do you think you're demanding of yourself, looking back?

[*Having given Emily two options going forward and here having chosen the healthier option, I then help her to identify the rigid attitude that underpins the unhealthier option.*]

Emily: … I think I'm probably attempting to demand perfection and to get everything right first time, which, now that I look at it, is an impossibility and also definitely not anything that I would expect of my daughters or anyone else that I know, actually.

Windy: So, you're demanding perfection. Do you feel resentful about that part of you that was scared and doubtful and didn't stand forward?

Emily: Yeah.

Windy: And, when you're in that resentful frame of mind towards that part of yourself, what are you demanding there about yourself?

Emily: That I should've been better somehow... But, now that...

Windy: Better in what sense, Emily?

Emily: ... [*Long pause*] I'm not sure I can really answer that because now what I've realised is that I'm looking back on it without... really remembering the full extent of the situation and what I was having to deal with.

Windy: Yeah. It sounds like you have some kind of ideal image of yourself.

Emily: Yeah.

Windy: 'The perfect anxiety-free Emily who shouldn't have put up with all this crap and shouldn't have wasted 16 years and wouldn't have been in that situation.'

Emily: Yes, I think so. ... Yeah.

Windy: I mean, my take on ideals, that there are two ways of dealing with ideals: one is to see them as a roadmap, as a pathway, not necessarily towards perfection but to say, 'Well, look, OK, this is where I'd like to be'; or to have the idea, 'No, no, no, no, I should already have been there. I shouldn't have been so frightened. I absolutely shouldn't have been not doing the things that I want to do,' and that resentful part of you is still going to come up. That's not the problem. It's how you respond, Emily, when it comes up. I'm not a great believer in eradicating anything about human experience, because we know that, if you try to eradicate things, then you're going to have a problem about your failure to eradicate them.

[*Here, I am emphasizing that Emily's problem is not her ideals but the rigid attitude that she holds towards her ideal. I also make the point that when she immediately reacts to the adversity of failing to live up to her ideal from the standpoint of a rigid attitude that is not the problem. What is a problem is revealed in how she responds to this reaction and that trying to eradicate the reaction is part of the problem, not part of the solution.*]

Emily: Yeah.

Windy: So, the next time you get into a situation and you find yourself thinking, 'No, I shouldn't have done this. I shouldn't have been so doubtful and afraid,' what are you going to do?

Emily: I think I probably do need to stop and be a little bit kinder to myself.

Windy: How would that sound?

Emily: I think I would say something along the lines of,… [*pause*] probably, 'Why don't you just take some time to look at what you have achieved and the obstacles that you have overcome?' just to maybe give myself a bit of grounding.

Windy: Yeah, and I also think that there is a space for wishing that you weren't as doubtful and afraid as you were, and that's the sad bit. I think there is room for sadness and regret. I don't necessarily think that the way to deal with that is to try to put yourself into just a positive mode.

Emily: No.

Windy: Do you see what I'm saying?

Emily: Yeah.

Windy: But to feel sad and regretful, wishing that you had
               had an opportunity to deal with those fears and
               doubts, because it sounds like you didn't have an
               opportunity to deal with them.

*[Often when people are constructing a healthy alternative to a
rigid or extreme attitude, they overlook the constructiveness of
experiencing a healthy negative emotion about an adversity
such as failing to live up to an ideal.]*

Emily: No, that's true. I hadn't thought of it like that
               before, actually, and I think that's probably why
               everything sort of feels like it's come to a head
               over the last two or three years, because I'm now
               taking those steps to achieving the goals that I
               really want to achieve and I am having to confront
               them and it's been a bit overwhelming, to be
               honest. But, no, again, I do like the idea of looking
               back on it and giving myself a bit of a breathing
               space and going, 'I just wasn't given the
               opportunity to deal with things that perhaps maybe
               other 20-something year olds and through their 30s
               managed to wrestle with and to deal with.'

Windy: And, also, 'I wish that I maybe had dealt with
               myself then in the same way as I would deal with
               my daughters now.'

Emily: Yeah. It is something that I'm actively trying to do
               with them, but I think I'm forgetting to do it with
               myself, actually.

Windy: Right.

Emily: Yeah.

Windy: So, what would help you to take that reminder to
               help you to do that?

Emily: I think that probably, when I'm having those massive feelings of self-doubt and worrying about failing at something, whatever failing is, just to take myself back into mum mode and go, 'OK, well, if this was my daughter, what is it that I would be saying to her if she came to me with these kinds of things?'

[Here, Emily states that going into 'mum' mode would be helpful here so that she can be 'mum' to the part of her that is experiencing self-doubt and worry.]

Windy: Yeah, and, also, I think tonight what we're doing is, in a way, like a single session, just focusing on one, and what I'd suggest that you to do is, we've been focusing on your resentfulness about yourself in the past, maybe, once you've really taken that and put that into practice, maybe down the line you can come back and volunteer for another one so we could really focus on your self-doubt, because it sounds like that is also an area that you could actually usefully use.

So, listen, why don't you summarise, Emily, what you've got from this evening?

[Again inviting the person to summarise is a part of the process.]

Emily: I think I've made a connection about how I remember the situation isn't necessarily truthful. I think I focus too much on ideals rather than actually what's actually in front of me. And that one of the techniques that I could use to help me with all of that and to work through whatever issues I've got, to think of myself advising one of my daughters with how they could perhaps cope in a similar situation.

Windy: And then apply it to yourself.

Emily: Yeah.

Windy: But don't forget to create a space for looking back and to feel sad and disappointed that you wished you were able to be able to focus on your doubts a little earlier, and also the resentful part will still come up. That's not the problem, it's how you deal with it.

[*I sometimes add to the person's summary when they have omitted a salient point.*]

Emily: Yeah, no, that makes sense.

Windy: Is there anything you haven't said you'd like to say before we finish?

Emily: No, I don't think so. Thank you very much. It's been very useful. Very useful indeed.

Windy: Thank you very much, Emily. Take care.

Emily: Thank you.

7

Helping the Person to Deal with Anxiety by Relinquishing His Need for a Guarantee

Windy–Jaspreet Interview on 04/01/21
Time: 25 minutes 33 secs

Windy: OK, Jaspreet, we have 25 minutes together, how would you like to use the time?

Jaspreet: Yeah. First of all, thanks a lot. Just a quick background: my name is Jaspreet, I am 40 years old from India, New Delhi, married, blessed with two kids. And, on the issue side, what I just want to explain to you is I'm facing anxiety issues for the last almost 10 years. It is basically the fear factor involved with my job. I always fear that I will lose it for unknown reasons. Connected to that, I feel that I will not be able to feed my family properly because of the loss of a job and I'm not able to be successful in my life. Connected to this point, with the COVID issue, my current job I have a limited timeframe of three months and, unfortunately, I am not able to get new opportunities right now. So, in this situation right now, I'm even more tense that I'm not able to survive because of this issue.

Relating to that, I sometimes feel that, because of this anxiety issue, my performance does lack – I have a poor performance because of these anxiety issues in my job.

Windy: OK. So, if we were to deal with the one thing that would make the most difference to you with your anxiety, which would that be?

[Jaspreet has given a lot of information and it is important that I help him to focus on one issue.]

Jaspreet: I think one thing would be if I was able to control the fear factor. Actually, in some ways I keep on searching for the guarantee that there will be no loss of job, there will be no poverty. Because of these guarantees, I have been suffering for the last ten years.

Windy: Right, OK. By the way, let me just ask you a question: if you knew for certain, if we guaranteed you that, even if you lost your job, you'd still be able to feed your family, you wouldn't be successful, you wouldn't have a job, but you would be able to feed your family, would that make a difference to you?

Jaspreet: Yes, that would make a difference to me.

Windy: How big a difference to you?

Jaspreet: Because the reason is that I'm basically, as a main earner of the family, I want my children to be more secure and to have the financial thing there to secure their education, their schooling.

Windy: OK. So, it seems to me, Jaspreet, that you've got security around the wrong way, right?

Jaspreet: OK.

Windy: And you're very dedicated – you've been looking for guarantees for ten years now, but you've had ten years of anxiety, it sounds like. So, do you think there's a relationship between your relationship with guarantees and your anxiety?

[Often people say that in order to feel secure that need to have a guarantee. However, it is the need for a guarantee that leads to anxiety.]

Jaspreet: Earlier, I did not have the self-realisation of this fact. I was considering that my anxieties were fair enough, always fair, but now I relate that there is a relationship between the guarantee as well as the anxiety.

Windy: Right. Let's be clear and, incidentally, if you get this right for yourself, then you can be a good teacher to your kids, because it's no good teaching your kids that security is in money because that ain't gonna work, right?

Jaspreet: OK.

Windy: So, let me see if I understand you correctly. You start off with a desire: that you would like to have a guarantee that you wouldn't lose your job, for example. Is that correct? Is that what you'd like, a guarantee that you wouldn't lose your job?

Jaspreet: Yes, that's correct.

Windy: OK. So, listen, don't change that. Don't change that, Jaspreet, because that's a good desire to have, right?

[I often make this point to people. It is not their desire that is at the core of their emotional problem. If is their transformation of their desire into a rigid attitude that is at its core.]

Jaspreet: OK.

Windy: And don't lie to yourself saying it doesn't matter, because it does matter to you.

Jaspreet: Yes, it does matter to me.

Windy: Your desire for a guarantee is not the problem. Now, let me show you, OK?

Jaspreet: OK.

Windy: Now, I'm going to outline two attitudes and you can tell me which leads to healthy concern and which leads to unhealthy anxiety, OK?

Jaspreet: OK.

Windy: OK. So, here's the first attitude and it is what I call the 'R' attitude. Can you see that?

[I am showing Jaspreet a piece of paper with a large 'R' which stands for 'rigid'.]

Jaspreet: Yes, I can see that.

Windy: Can you see it's got 'R' on it, right?

Jaspreet: Yes.

Windy: OK, and the reason why it's got 'R' on it is going to be apparent. The 'R' attitude is: 'I would like to have a guarantee that I'm not going to lose my job and therefore I have to have that guarantee. I can't bear not having the guarantee.' That's the 'R' attitude, right?

Jaspreet: OK.

Windy: Now, the 'F' attitude – you see that?

[*Now, I am showing Jaspreet a piece of paper with a large 'F', which stands for flexible.*]

Jaspreet: Yes, I can see that.

Windy: Good. I'm going to have to get more professional ones done. So, Matt, if you're listening, just send me nice 'R's and 'F's through the post and I'll be grateful. Anyway, you've got the 'F' attitude, and the 'F' attitude is this: 'Again, I'd like to have a guarantee, but sadly and regretfully I don't have to have it and, while not having it is unfortunate, it's not terrible,' right?

Jaspreet: OK.

Windy: Now, be honest with yourself, which attitude underpins your anxiety: the 'F' or the 'R'?

Jaspreet: … I think logically–

Windy: No, no, no, whoa, whoa, whoa. Not logically. I'm talking about when you're anxious which attitude underpins your anxiety?

[*In helping a person distinguish between their rigid attitude and their flexible attitude, I stress the importance of them doing so when they are experiencing an unhealthy negative emotion such as anxiety.*]

Jaspreet: It's 'R'.

Windy: Yes, it's 'R'. Correct, it's 'R'. Now, Jaspreet, what difference would it make to you in your life if you changed 'R' to 'F', changing from, 'I must have a guarantee that I'm not going to lose my job and it's terrible if I don't have the guarantee,' to, 'I'd like to have a guarantee that I'm not going to lose my job, but I don't need one. It would be unfortunate if I don't have a guarantee but not the end of the world'? What would your life be like if you had the 'F' attitude?

Jaspreet: OK, I will be able to deal with my anxiety I would say more confidently. It's about desire: there should be a guarantee.

Windy: You've got to make a distinction, Jaspreet. Very important to make a distinction between your desire, which is present in both attitudes, right?

Jaspreet: Right.

Windy: And, in one case, you're turning your desire into a demand, into a rigid demand and, in the other one, you're keeping it flexible, right?

Jaspreet: Yes.

Windy: So, don't see that your desire equals your 'should' because it's separate and that's really important. Now, the 'R' stands for Rigid and the 'F' stands for Flexible.

Jaspreet: OK.

Windy: So, at the moment, you've got the Rigid and we're trying to encourage you to get the Flexible. Now, how do you do this? At the first sign that you're anxious, ask yourself, 'Is my attitude based on I must have a guarantee or I'd like one but I don't need one?' The quicker you can intervene with yourself, the better, because, if you're anxious and then you start looking for guarantees and doing all the things that you do, that you've done in the past just to try to make sure that you're safe, the real safety, Jaspreet, is in your flexible attitude. Now, which attitude do you think you'd want to teach your kids, for example?

[Quite often, people like Jaspreet are not clear in making the distinction between a rigid attitude and a flexible attitude and so, my task is to help them to do this.]

Jaspreet: 'F', I would say.

Windy: Yeah. Now, let's hear you do it. Your kids come to you and say to you, 'Dad, we need to be financially secure. We have to know that we're going to be financially secure in the future,' what are you going to say to them?

[Here I am inviting Jaspreet to rehearse his flexible attitude by imagining that he is teaching this attitude to his children.]

Jaspreet: That's a tough one, I would say. Obviously, I would say that there is no guarantee; that you can be financially secure, but you can try your level best within your limitations so that you can be financially secure and, if you could not be, then still it's OK. At least you have the money to survive whatever the basic needs you have. So, I will try to explain to them in such a manner.

Windy: OK, but the one thing that you need to explain to them and explain to yourself is the solution to your anxiety is not showing yourself there are no guarantees, right?

Jaspreet: OK.

Windy: The solution is recognising that you would like
them but you don't need them, right?

*[This is another important distinction. People with an anxiety
problem that stems from a need for a guarantee think that the
solution to this problem is to remind themselves that there is
no guarantee. It is not. As I make clear to Jaspreet, the
solution is to acknowledge that he would like a guarantee, but
that he does not need one.]*

Jaspreet: OK, I've got it.

Windy: You see, the solution to my problems about my
lack of hair is not that I've got lack of hair, the
solution is that I'd like to have hair but I don't
need it.

Jaspreet: OK.

Windy: You got it?

Jaspreet: OK, I got it.

Windy: Alright. So, let me teach you and the group Albert
Ellis' Money Model, since we're talking about
money and it's very relevant to this. I'm going to
teach you and the group the Money Model just in
case they haven't encountered it because it's quite
a good one. Are you ready?

*[In order to underscore the point I have made to Jaspreet, I
decide to use a teaching device developed by Albert Ellis
called the 'Money Model'. This model makes clearly
distinguishes between a flexible attitude and a rigid attitude
and outlines their differential consequences.]*

Jaspreet: Ready.

Windy: OK. In your currency, how much is £10 sterling?

Jaspreet: It's 1,000 INR.

Windy: How do you pronounce it?

Jaspreet: It's Indian rupees. 1,000 INR.

Windy: Do you mind if I call them Indian rupees?

Jaspreet: Yeah, rupees, that's fine.

Windy: So, there are different parts of the model. Now, pay close attention. Part 1: you would like, at all times, to have 1,000 rupees in your pocket, right?

Jaspreet: OK.

Windy: Your attitude is, 'I'd like to have 1,000 rupees on me at all times, but I don't need to have them,' alright?

Jaspreet: OK.

Windy: Now, you look in your pocket and you've got 900 rupees. You want 1,000. You don't need it but you want it and you've got 900. Now, how do you feel?

Jaspreet: … [*Pause*] OK, my feeling would be that, since I need 1,000 rupees…

Windy: No, didn't say 'need'. You see, you've invented the 'need'. This is where you'd better be very clear. I'm not saying 'need' and you're showing very nicely, Jaspreet how human beings find it very difficult to keep flexible and rigid ideas separate. I said that you would like to have a minimum of 1,000 rupees.

[*Once again Jaspreet is showing that he has not quite grasped the distinction that he needs to grasp in order to solve his problem.*]

Jaspreet: 1,000 rupees, OK.

Windy: You don't have to have it. You don't need it.

Jaspreet: I'd like to have it.

Windy: But it would be good to have, right?

Jaspreet: OK.

Windy: Good to have, you don't need it. Now, you've got 900. How do you feel?

Jaspreet: … [*Long pause*] Since I'd like to have 1,000 but have only 900, I would say it's fine with me.

Windy: No, it's not fine. You see, this is another thing that human beings do to themselves. They say, 'Well, I haven't got what I want. It's fine.' It's not. It matters to you, right? So, I would say that you would feel either disappointed or you'd feel concerned. Is that correct?

[*In answer to my question, Jaspreet says that it is fine if he does not get his desire met. REBT theory argues that it is not fine; rather, it is unfortunate or disappointing.*]

Jaspreet: Yeah, I would feel concerned.

Windy: Yeah, but you wouldn't be anxious, right?

Jaspreet: Yeah, I will not be anxious.

Windy: Good, but you'd be concerned and that's good because that tells you that you've got to do some things, like figure out how you're going to get another 100 rupees. Now, Part 2 of the model is this, Jaspreet: this time you've still got the desire to have a minimum of 1,000 rupees at all times, right?

Jaspreet: OK.

Windy: But this time you say that you have to have it. You must. It's absolutely essential to have that, OK?

Jaspreet: OK.

Windy: And, again, you look in your purse and you've got 900 rupees and you're really saying, 'I've got to have 1,000, a minimum of 1,000. It's absolutely essential. It's terrible if I don't.' Now how do you feel?

Jaspreet: I will feel disappointed. I would say I'm not having 1,000 rupees. A little feeling of dissatisfaction would be the essence. I must have 1,000 rupees. So, in the second Part B, the feeling will be a little disappointed, I would say.

[Yet again, Jaspreet shows that he is not grasping the relationship between anxiety and a rigid attitude. Note that I am persistent on this point.]

Windy: You see, again, it's very interesting: when I'm actually emphasising your 'must', you don't seem to see that, if you really believed that, you'd be very anxious.

Jaspreet: Yeah, obviously.

Windy: Well, no, not obviously. You see, again, partly your problem is, and this is a universal problem, that we don't make key discriminations between two things: one is our attitudes and two is our feelings, OK?

Jaspreet: OK.

Windy: Now, which of those two is going to lead to anxiety: the idea that you'd like to have a minimum of 1,000 rupees but you don't need it or that you absolutely need it; that it's terrible if you don't? Which of those attitudes is going to lead you to be anxious when you've got 900 and you're, on one case, demanding that you have to have 1,000? Which attitude's going to lead to anxiety?

Jaspreet: I understand. It's obviously the 'must'.

Windy: That's right. Now, the third part of the model is this: you're still believing that you absolutely have to have a minimum of 1,000 rupees at all times, right? You're anxious because you've got 900 and then you find, to your amazement, that you missed 200 rupees that you had in your top pocket. Now you've got 1,100. Now how do you feel?

Jaspreet: … [*Pause*] I would feel happy since I have more than what my requirement is. I would feel more happy.

Windy: Right. You will be happy or relieved.

Jaspreet: Yeah.

Windy: But you still believe that you absolutely have to have a minimum of 1,000 rupees at all times. Now you've got 1,100 and then a thought occurs to you that leads you to be very anxious again. What do you think that would be?

Jaspreet: Sorry, can you come again? I was not able to connect.

Windy: I'm saying you've got 1,100 and you're pleased and you're happy. You're still believing that you have to have a minimum of 1,000 at all times. You've now got 1,100 and you're happy. You're still believing that you have to have a minimum of 1,000 at all times and some thought occurs to you that leads you to be very anxious again. What would it be?

Jaspreet: It would be like..., I think, because of the worry factor, maybe because of my constant thinking that I should have a minimum of 1,000 rupees, I will be still having that feeling of anxiousness in my mind.

Windy: Because you've got 1,100 and you're happy, but then something occurs to you. Now, what occurs to you that leads you to be anxious again?

Jaspreet   Yes, I will still be anxious.

Windy: But why? Why would you be anxious?

Jaspreet: ... [*Pause*] Why I will be anxious? Maybe... [*pause*] because of the nature of the thinking, that anxiety factor or consciousness inbuilt in my own mind.

Windy: Yes, but you still have to think about some threat, you see. This type of thinking you need some threat. Now, what could happen to you? You've got 1,100 rupees, you're demanding a minimum of 1,000 and you're happy and then you think that something might happen that would lead you to be anxious. What might happen to you that would lead you to be anxious?

[*It would be easy for me to give Jaspreet the correct answer, but I am still trying to encourage him to figure it out for himself.*]

Jaspreet: Yeah. Maybe, again, the fear factor – maybe I lose the money in the future.

Windy: Exactly. Brilliant. You've got it. 'Maybe I lose something,' right?

Jaspreet: Yes.

Windy: So, that's the point. Human beings, black or white, rich or poor, female, male, it doesn't matter, whichever part, when they hold a rigid attitude towards something, they're anxious in case they don't have their rigid demands met, but they're still underlyingly anxious when they do have their rigid demands met because now you've got the money but how do you know you're not going to lose it or what's going to happen tomorrow. So, true security is not having a job almost, because you're saying, 'I want a guarantee that I'm going to have a job.' You've been looking in the wrong place. True security is in your mind, which is free, you see?

Jaspreet: Yeah.

Windy: Now, if you really get these discriminations, and, again, if you write to me, we'll send you the recording so you can really go over it and get these discriminations, you can see how difficult you found, until the end, to see the differences between these types of attitudes and the feelings that they engender. If you really work at that and teach your children, both you and your children would be healthily concerned but unanxious, because both of you would be saying, 'We would like a guarantee that everything's going to be fine, but we don't need one.'

Jaspreet: OK.

Windy: Because at the moment you're saying, 'We need one,' and, even if we give you one, you'd say, 'Yeah, but how do we know that the guarantee's going to last? It might not last,' you see. So, needing a guarantee leads to insecurity.

Jaspreet: Yes.

Windy: And the cure for psychological insecurity is not money, it's not a job. It's changing your attitude.

Jaspreet: … Yes. … I understand that. Thanks a lot, first of all, for giving a very clear explanation.

Windy: Yeah.

Jaspreet: But I have one question: practically, this concept, how can he implement it into his day-to-day life?

Windy: By following Albert Ellis' question: whenever your anxious, ask yourself the question, 'What am I demanding?' and, once you know the kinds of things that you're demanding, which for you is a guarantee, as soon as you're anxious, you say, 'Am I demanding a guarantee?' and you've got to be honest with yourself – 'Yes, I am.' Now, then you say, 'Well, look, I have a choice: I can either continue to demand a guarantee or I can really show myself I'd like it but I don't need it.' Which is the one that's true in the world? How does the world work? You see, if the world worked on the idea that, as long as you're demanding a guarantee, we'd give you one, you wouldn't be here talking to me. You'd be quite happy having a guarantee. If the world worked when I say I must have hair and it grew, then musts would be consistent with reality. Are they?

Jaspreet: OK, got it.

Windy: The other thing is which is healthier? 'What would I teach my children?' – that's a real important one. Would I teach my children: 'Come kids, let me teach you how to be anxious,' or, 'Come, kids, let me teach you how to be concerned but not anxious'? Which one would you teach your kids? And then you'd teach it to yourself, but you've got to work towards really intervening with yourself as quickly as you can. There's no magic. There's nothing that you can say. I often say I can teach a parrot to sound rational and healthy but I can't teach a parrot to be rational and healthy. Human beings are blessed with the ability to think about their thinking.

Jaspreet: OK.

Windy: So, read some of my writings, read some of Dr Ellis' writings and really show yourself that, if you really work at this steadily, don't go crazy, that you could make a profound difference to yourself in a short period of time and that you wouldn't be practising how to be anxious for the last 10 years, because that's what you've been doing.

Jaspreet: Thank you very much for the explanation.

Windy: OK.

Jaspreet: I have got the idea.

Windy: Good.

Jaspreet: That's wonderful, yeah.

Windy: OK. Thank you very much and now we'll take some questions.

[As discussed earlier in the book, I record these brief therapeutic conversations and encourage volunteers to write to me to get a copy if they wish. I will also send them a transcript of the session if they request it. I encouraged Jaspreet to get the recording from me because he has struggled to grasp the important distinctions that REBT makes between flexible and rigid attitudes and between attitudes at B in the ABC model and emotions at C. If he does not make and use these distinctions, he will not solve his problem in the longer term.]

8

Helping a Person to Develop Flexibility and Patience When Starting a New Job

Windy–Kate Interview on 21/12/20
Time: 17 minutes 36 secs

Windy: OK, Kate, what's your understanding of the purpose of our conversation today?

Kate: So, my understanding is that, through some discussion with you, you will enable me to maybe solve a problem that I bring to the session.

Windy: I will do my level best. I'll roll up my sleeves if you roll your sleeves up at the same time.

Kate: Absolutely. Ready.

Windy: Excellent. Let's go. What problem do you have?

Kate: OK, so, I've started a new job about three weeks, which is it's always difficult starting a new job. I've moved house. And, in a supervision session in my first couple of weeks, my supervisor gave some, well, constructive feedback, really, which I took quite badly and, having reflected upon it, I feel that this sort of perceived criticism is something that tends to pervade all areas of my life.

Windy: What do you do for a living?

Kate: I'm a CBT therapist.

Windy: OK, well, that's alright.

Kate: So, I should be able to deal, and that's part of it as well – I think I feel I should be able to deal with that.

Windy: Well, OK, we'll come to that, but I'm assuming that you're human first well before being a CBT therapist.

Kate: Yeah.

Windy: Therefore, not immune from the vagaries of human problems.

Kate: No.

Windy: OK. So, it sounds like you got some feedback which part of you sees as constructive but another part of you reacted in a different way. Is that right?

Kate: Yeah.

Windy: Now, if we could just focus on that part of you, what was that part of you feeling in response to the feedback?

Kate: So, really, I was catastrophising because I think that my first thought was, 'Oh, I knew I was no good at this job and I'll get found out if I change my job and they'll realise I can't do my job, so I'll lose my job, then I'd lose my house.' So, it was that catastrophic thinking, that I felt threatened by it.

Windy: I mean, don't stop there: you'll end up on the streets, you'll be a bag lady.

Kate: Absolutely, yeah.

Windy: Let's do the whole hog.

[*I am humorously going along with her awfulising to demonstrate understanding.*]

Kate: Yeah.

Windy: So, it sounds like you brought to the job the idea that you weren't going to be any good at it anyway and you'd be found out quickly. Is that right?

Kate: Yeah. Yeah, I've always thought that.

Windy: Yeah. You mean you've always thought that about anything you've done?

Kate: Pretty much, yeah. I think that is the thing, I'm not good enough. I don't feel good enough for anything.

Windy: And what happens when you get into a job? Does that feeling go or how does it work?

Kate: No, I think it's worse initially because I think that I get into panic mode and I'll be overpreparing everything to make sure that they don't find out that I'm not good enough.

Windy: OK. So, what for you would convince you at the beginning of a job – let's take this job: you've moved house, you've started a new job – what would you need to have in terms of either external or internal conditions that would lead you to conclude that you were good enough to do the job?

Kate: Externally, I tend to need a lot of feedback and I need praise quite a lot. Internally, I guess would be... I would need to have some self-belief.

Windy: Belief about what?

Kate: That I am able to do the things that I have to do or need to do.

Windy: Right. So, in a sense, with those internal conditions, you would need to know right from the start that you were able to do it, right?

Kate: Yeah.

Windy: And, if you don't have that conviction right at the start, what do you then conclude?

Kate: That I can't do it.

[*This is a common dynamic; 'I must know right from the start that I can do x' and I don't know this then I can't do it'. A little later, Kate shows the 'now' time dimension of this rigid attitude.*]

Windy: Right. So, there's no place for you starting a job saying, 'Look, I don't know at the moment whether I'm going to be able to do this job or not. Let's see.'

Kate: Yeah. I am very impatient.

Windy: Right. So, you need to know that you can do it when?

Kate: Right now.

Windy: Immediately.

Kate: Yeah.

Windy: And, if you don't have it right now, then you're not going to be any good at it. OK.

Kate: Yeah.

Windy: So, again, you start off, it sounds like, with a good preference as well, which is, 'Look, I would like to know,' – let's leave the external conditions because I don't think that's a central part of your problem, it then becomes part of the problem, but I think I'm going to leave that, if that's OK, just for a moment to one side.

[It would have been better if I confirmed this with Kate rather than make a unilateral decision on this point.]

Kate: Yeah.

Windy: So, you start off with a preference which says something like this, just on this particular job: 'I would like to know immediately that I can do it,' and there's nothing wrong with that as long as you make it flexible, right?

[By now you will probably realise that this is one of my standard interventions. I begin with a person's preference – in this case 'I would like to know immediately that I can do it' – and then validate this preference. The rest of the steps are below. I call this method, 'Windy's Review Assessment Procedure (WRAP).]

Kate: Yeah.

Windy: Which sounds like what? How would that sound if you were flexible about it?

Kate: Well, if I was flexible, I guess I would say to myself, 'It's early days. You've only just started the job. Actually, give it a little bit of time to be able to get used to everything, the changes.'

Windy: Well, no, actually, that misses the mark.

Kate: OK.

Windy: Because the real flexibility – again, I think you're trying to help yourself in a similar way by not getting to the core of the issue, and the core of the issue is your desire, which you then turn into what we might say is a demanding impatience. 'I'd like to know that I can do it straight away and, therefore, I have to,' as opposed to, 'I'd like to be able to do it straight away, but I don't have to have that conviction.' Now, which do you hold? Which do you bring with you to any job? The rigid way?

[Because Kate is a little unclear about what constitutes a flexible attitude, I outline both the flexible attitude (preference with the demand negated) and the rigid attitude (preference with the demand asserted) and ask her which attitude she brings to her new job. Outlining these two attitudes is the next step of the WRAP.]

Kate: The first one, yeah.

Windy: And what would happen if you brought the more flexible attitude towards your job?

[The next step in using the WRAP is asking the person how they would respond if they held a the flexible attitude in the situation in which they currently hold the rigid attitude.]

Kate: I guess it would put less pressure on me.

Windy: Yeah, and then you'd be able to take advantage of what you then were trying to tell yourself, which is, 'Look, this is a new job, etc., etc.,' but, if you try and tell yourself those things without dealing with your real problem, then it's not going to make any difference. Now, my hypothesis then is, when you don't change that rigid must, you then really rely on other people to give you praise, right?

[I make two important points here. First, if Kate were to hold her flexible attitude to beginning a new job then she would <u>then</u> be able to utilise the self-talk she outlined above (i.e. 'It's early days. You've only just started the job. Actually, give it a little bit of time to be able to get used to everything, the changes'). However, when she holds her rigid attitude, she is not able to be guided by this type of thinking until she changes it to a flexible attitude. The second point that I make here is that when she hold a rigid attitude towards herself she then relies upon external validation to give praise etc.]

Kate: Yeah.

Windy: What did they say to you, the part of you that thought was constructive? What did they say to you?

Kate: The thing that triggered this?

Windy: Yeah, in supervision. Part of you said it was constructive, so what did they say to you?

Kate: Well, initially, my reaction was that it was negative because she questioned my rationale and for using an intervention and also my client goals – they weren't smart enough. So, that immediately said to me, 'Oh, you've not done it well enough,' but, when I actually reflected on it afterwards, I was able to see that they weren't, because I looked into it, I read up on it a little bit. So, it has improved my practice.

Windy: Right.

Kate: So, I've tried to reframe it as, 'This is constructive and it's enabled me to develop,' as opposed to that initial threat.

Windy: So, you would like a supervisor to really say, 'This is fantastic. This is fantastic. This is great. This is wonderful,' right? You would like one of those.

Kate: Yeah. But it's not realistic.

Windy: No, but actually that's what you're looking for as long as you don't deal with that internal idea. Now, listen, we could have two narratives here, Kate. One is, 'I'm Kate and, whenever I start a new job, I have to know straight away that I can do it well, otherwise I don't think I'll ever do it well. I'm an imposter and, therefore, I need people to tell me how great I am.' That's narrative number one.

Kate: Yeah.

Windy: Narrative number two is: 'Hi, I'm Kate, and of course I'd like to know I can do it straight away, but I don't have to know, for God's sake. This is a new thing. I really don't have to know, and not knowing that I won't be able to do it doesn't mean that I won't be able to do it. It just means I don't know. So, I'm going to go forward with that idea and, therefore, I'll be able to take supervisory comments, which are not wonderfulising my work, in my stride.' Now, you can practise either of those narratives, Kate.

Kate: ... [*Pause*] Yeah.

Windy: Which one do you want to practise?

[*I sometimes like to outline two narratives. One, in this case is based on Kate's rigid attitude and the other is based on her flexible attitude. A narrative outlines the person's attitude and details its effects. I then ask a person which narrative they would like to take forward and practise.*]

Kate: The second one.

Windy: Yeah. Incidentally, you don't need any practice to do the first one.

Kate: Yeah, I've been doing it all my life.

Windy: You're pretty good at that. But you could actually, right now, start a new narrative for Kate, but that means watching out for the old one starting now, because that's what happens with narratives. You're kind of, 'No, wait a minute, I know what's going on here. I'm starting to feel like an imposter. I know what's going on in here. It's my demand that I have to know right now that I can do it.'

[*The first point of change is awareness of the beginning of the problem. The second is using this awareness to look for the rigid or extreme attitude that underpins the problem.*]

Kate: Yeah.

Windy: And then you really deal with that, but don't get rid of the desire because every morning I get up in the morning and I say, 'Look, I'd like hair.'

There's nothing wrong with that desire as long as I
keep it flexible. And then you'll be more likely to
calm down and not be so reliant on external and
then you'll be able to give yourself more internal
things. So, do you think you'll be able to do that?

[*The third point is to have the person validate their preference
but to negate the demand. I could have been more specific in
outlining Kate's flexible attitude here.*]

Kate: … I can try.

Windy: I'm not asking you to try, Kate. I don't like 'try's,
somebody says, 'I'll try.'

[*As Yoda in Star Wars says, 'Do. Or do not. There is no try.'*]

Kate: So, once the feeling starts to come up, that I am an
imposter, be more flexible in my attitude that
actually I don't need to know that I'm going to be
OK at it; it's OK not to know.

[*When doing a brief single session of REBT, I could
theoretically pick up on more issues but choose to let some go.
I sometime pick a person up on their use of 'OK'. Thus, I could
have pointed out to Kate that it's actually 'not OK' not to
know, it is undesirable not to know since this better reflects her
flexible attitude. However, I chose to let it go because in the
course of the session it was, in my view, peripheral not
central.*]

Windy: Yeah. Albert Ellis would say to you, 'As soon as
the imposter feelings come up, cherchez le should,
cherchez le must' – look for what demands you're
making and your demand is, 'I must know right
now that I can do it,' and, because you don't, you
flip over to the other side, because that's the black
and white, 'and I'll never be able to do it and,

therefore, the only way I can survive is to get the external praise.'

Kate: Yeah.

Windy: So, right from the start. So, don't worry if the imposter feelings come up, don't worry if you get negative reactions to supervision, because these reactions are telling you or informing you that you're under the influence of a 'must' and you need to question it.

[I often tell the person that their initial reactions are signs that they are 'under the influence' of a rigid/extreme attitude and they can use this reaction to respond more constructively to this attitude.]

Kate: … [Pause] Yeah.

Windy: Alright?

Kate: Yeah.

Windy: And I think, if you do that, you'll be able to take forward a new narrative for Kate.

Kate: Yeah. It's definitely to do with it, with the impatience. I guess it is about not knowing. I think that's what it is, isn't it, because I am very impatient with anything. If I try it and I don't do it well the first time, I give up.

Windy: That's right. But, again, having a desire to do it straight away is not the problem. It's whether you convert that into a demand or whether you keep it flexible. Now, incidentally, you mentioned that being a CBT therapist might make things a little worse for you. Were you saying that tongue in cheek or do you have that idea that, because you're a CBT therapist, you should be able to deal with this yourself, or what?

Kate: Yeah, that is the kind of feeling. It feels a bit embarrassing that I'm not able to do that myself when I know that I talk to clients on a daily basis with similar thoughts and feelings. It just seems so difficult for me to do.

Windy: Yeah, and of course, with your clients, when they come in and you say, 'Look, do this,' and they come back and they say, 'I'm struggling,' you say, 'You're struggling? You haven't done it straight away yet?'

Kate: Yeah.

Windy: 'You'll never be able to do it.'

Kate: So, I'm putting those conditions onto them as well, yeah.

Windy: Yeah. Well, the point is you're not. You don't do that with your clients, do you?

Kate: Well, I don't know. I probably am a little bit impatient sometimes with them, yeah.

Windy: Yeah.

Kate: Possibly, yeah.

Windy: It would be nice if all clients were dedicated to doing their homework and doing things well, but do they have to be that way?

Kate: … No. I mean, I do have quite a good success rate, so I'm doing something right, I know that.

Windy: That's right, or you can go into private practice and have up on your website: 'I only accept clients who assiduously do their homework quickly. If you don't do that, go find somebody else.'

[Interestingly, Kate to some degree also has that same demanding attitude towards her clients. Although we did not discuss it, my hypothesis is that she views her clients' success as evidence that she is doing a good job that keeps her self-demand at bay. Note the humour in my last response. Again, I find humour a good way of casting doubt on a person's rigid/extreme attitude.]

Kate: Yeah.

Windy: Alright, listen, why don't you sum up the work we've done today?

Kate: So, I put a lot of demands on myself to do things quickly and well. So, I need to be a little bit more flexible in my view around not knowing what's going to happen in order to not be a slave to those demands – those 'shoulds' and 'musts'. That's what I understand.

Windy: Yeah, that's right. And, as I say, if you recognise that these old feelings are going to come up because you're still holding to those underlying demands and the feelings are a sign that you need to catch those demands, bring them out, examine them and then really go forward with the more flexible ones, and the more you do that and the more you allow yourself to do it at a speed that you can do it, as opposed to the speed that you would insist that you do it, because it might be a quc stion of more haste less speed when you put those impatient demands on yourself.

Kate: Yeah.

Windy: So, if you allow yourself to do it at your speed – it would be nice if it was quicker, but it doesn't have to be – and you did it steadily, then, if you commit yourself, then you don't have to commit yourself to trying. You can commit yourself to doing.

Kate: Yeah.

Windy: Is there anything else that we haven't covered that you'd like to cover before we've finished on this particular point?

Kate: No, I don't think so, because I think that that does, like I say, pervade every area of my life but it's the same core belief.

Windy: Yeah, and, therefore, as I said, to reduce it, you can actually take this core belief and then you can, again, look for it when your feelings are indicating that it's started to bubble up to the surface.

[Here I am suggesting that Kate can take what we discussed and use here flexible attitude in other areas of her life.]

Kate: Yeah. Yeah.

Windy: OK, good.

Kate: Thank you.

Windy: Well, listen, let me wish you good luck on that, OK?

Kate: Thank you very much. Yeah.

Windy: OK, then.

9

Helping the Person to See that Only She Can Do It, But She Doesn't Have to Do It Alone

Windy–Raniya: Interview on 02/12/20
Time: 14 minutes 53 secs

Windy: OK, Raniya, what problem do you have that you'd like some help with?

Raniya: Well, the nature of my problem is a little bit complex and I would like to share it with you and to be able to find some solution, because I am trying to find a solution for quite a period of time. Basically, my husband, we are living separately currently, and I have a son and he's nine years old and, almost for a one-year period, he's still unable to grasp the concept and this is emotionally disturbing him and he is showing the behaviour of nail-biting as well. And I have tried to recover him from it, but still he tries to talk it out sometimes. He's putting the same questions repetitively.

Windy: So, he can't grasp what concept?

Raniya: The only thing that is bothering him is, 'Why my father cannot be like the fathers that my friends have,' why he can't be like that, because he's observant and he is quite an intelligent child. So, when he observes the behaviour of other people and when he observes the behaviour of my brothers towards their families, that disturbs him, because he sees the difference between the families, and he has observed a lot of conflict in our marriage and relationship. So, sometimes, even when he questions me because my marriage was completely arranged, so he questions me why I even married that person, why I didn't think of it, and this is basically bothering me a lot, because I have no guilt. Whatever has happened, I am comfortable with it, but he's not able to manage.

Windy: How do you feel about your son's continual questioning? Is he upset about the situation?

Raniya: He is upset, although he wasn't very much attached to his father, but still he's upset.

Windy: Right. Because he sees that other people…

Raniya: This is the only thing that produces guilt in me, because I am a professional, I have tough timings – I have to work for eight hours or sometimes longer than that – and I feel like I am unable to manage him in this conflictive situation.

Windy: When you say 'unable to manage him', what do you mean?

Raniya: Unable to give him a good time, quality time, although, when I'm at home, I prefer not to do anything other than just talking to him, playing with him or focusing on him.

Windy: Right. So, you do give him care and attention when you're at home.

Raniya: Yes.

Windy: Yeah.

Raniya: That's my focal point.

Windy: But what would you like me to help you with today?

Raniya: I would like you to help me as to how I can help him overcome this issue, because his questions are always the same or similar.

Windy: OK. Well, let me tell you what I can do and what I can't do. I'm not a child psychologist, so I'm not really ethically able to give you some advice about your son because that's not my area of interest. I can help you deal with your emotional issues about your son.

[Transparency is important in single-session work so I made it clear to Raniya what I can do and cannot do in the time available.]

Raniya: It is giving me quite a challenge too, because I am juggling around many things and this is affecting my mental health now, because at the back of my mind I'm thinking about what he's thinking, what's happening with him. I have to juggle because my elder brother is not here, he lives in Dubai, so I have to look after my parents, I have to build the responsibility of my home as well, and I have to manage him. So, there are so many things.

Windy: Yeah, but let's focus on one thing that, if we could resolve today, it would give you a sense that things were moving forward, because I think part of the problem is that you keep bringing all of the problems together.

[As I note, Raniya is bringing a number of issues together which may be a factor explaining why she has not been able to help herself. I want to help her by encouraging her to focus on one thing.]

Raniya: That's the issue with me. That's the problem, because I am constantly thinking on so many things that it becomes a little bit hard to manage everything.

Windy: OK. In England, we say, if were you a horse, we'd put blinkers on you. They put blinkers on horses sometimes.

Raniya: Yes.

Windy: So, let's see if we can help you to really focus just on one particular problem. So, what one particular problem do you want to focus on today, in terms of your feelings?

Raniya: Yes, that concern with my feelings is, the only thing I think if I could focus on is being a little bit ignorant with the things and I can focus on being happy, because, when I'm thinking so much about everything, I am depressed. Although I'm smiling all the time, I feel as though there is some sort of emotional trauma laying underneath whatever I'm going through.

Windy: And what do you think that trauma is?

Raniya: Because I feel that I don't share my feelings with anyone, so, when I'm fearing and I'm just piling up, mostly it turns out as an anger burst without any reason. My blood pressure shoots. I react without any reason because I'm unable to manage that burst of powerful emotions.

Windy: OK. So, what kind of psychologist are you?

Raniya: I'm a clinical psychologist.

Windy: OK, so, you're a clinical psychologist who doesn't want to seek help for herself.

Raniya: Yeah, because I have discussed and I shared the same scenario, like taking....

Windy: Look, if I was to have a client, I'd say, 'Look, you need some help about this. You're doing it all on your own.' What I'm saying is what stops you from saying, 'Look, I need to work with somebody. I don't have to do it all on my own. I'm on my own, so maybe it's a good idea for me to have some help with somebody else'? What would stop you from doing that?

[Again note that Raniya does not nominate a specific issue, so from what she has said I am hypothesizing that her problems are being maintained by her refusal to seek help for them.]

Raniya: Because the one thing that I hate, that I don't like, is others sympathising with what happened to me. That's why the majority of people have no idea what happened to me.

Windy: Listen, but you could find an REBT therapist in India and they're not going to sympathise with you. REBT therapists won't give you any sympathy. They'll give you empathy, but they won't give you sympathy.

[Raniya fears that if she tells someone her problems that they will sympathise with her, which she abhors. I make the point that REB therapists will offer empathy and not sympathy.]

Raniya: Yes, I think that's a great idea, in fact.

Windy: Yeah, because at the moment you're saying, 'I can't go and see and talk about and get help because I can't bear the idea that somebody's going to feel sorry for me.'

Raniya: Yes, and that's the reason I don't share it with anyone, because I don't want anyone to be sympathetic towards me.

Windy: Yeah.

Raniya: It happened to me, it's none of your concern – that's my point of view: that's not your concern. It's my way.

Windy: But let's suppose that you were sure that, if you went to see somebody, they would help you and not feel sorry for you, would you go and see them?

Raniya: Yes, definitely.

Windy: So, you see, at the moment you've got this idea which is stopping you and, because you're not really opening up to anybody, you're keeping it all in your head and you're going from one thing to another. So, I think that, if you really show yourself, 'Now, listen, I can reach out to somebody else,' and you can tell them right from the start, 'Please don't sympathise with me,' right?

[Raniya has shown that she has an unbearability attitude towards others feeling sorry for her. I make the point that she can be open about not wanting sympathy for someone who could help her.]

Raniya: Yes.

Windy: Tell them right from the start: 'Don't sympathise with me. Help me without sympathy,' right?

Raniya: Yes.

Windy: And then have a session with them and, if they sympathise with you, you get rid of them and you go onto somebody else, right?

Raniya: Yes, it can be done.

Windy: Exactly.

Raniya: It's just a practical solution.

[*In a way, Raniya is correct. The emotional solution is for her to develop a bearability attitude towards receiving sympathy from others. However, she would still have a very strong preference about not being pitied. Consequently, I suggest that she could voice her strong preference for a pity-free response from a helper, have a session with the person and not return if she gets pity from that person. If she follows this suggestion, she will be seeking the help that would benefit her.*]

Windy: Right. And, also, the other thing is have you consulted a child psychologist about your son?

Raniya: … Well, I'm not sure about that because he is not sharing with anyone.

Windy: No, I'm not saying for him. I'm saying for you.

Raniya: Like I consult a child psychologist and take an opinion about how I should deal with him? Is this what you're suggesting?

Windy: Yeah. That's what I can't do for you because I'm not a child psychologist, child therapist. But I'm suggesting that, if you consulted a child therapist, child psychologist, they would be able to say to you things like, 'Well, that's perfectly natural,' etc., or, 'No, I think that needs attention.'

Raniya: Well, I have studied it, because, obviously, I have worked with a child over a period of time because my own interest area is child psychology.

Windy: I know that, but it's different having somebody else's opinion.

Raniya: It's a different situation.

Windy: Exactly, yeah.

Raniya: I'm unable to help him by myself, but I'm trying to, but I think it's difficult for me to manage him.

Windy: Well, because the other thing is you're trying to do everything on your own.

Raniya: Yes.

Windy: As opposed to reaching out and utilising the resources that you have available to you.

Raniya: Yes. I should.

Windy: Do you have this idea, 'If I have a problem, I've got to sort it out by myself'?

Raniya: By myself, yes.

Windy: Yeah.

[As I continue to have a conversation with Raniya, it becomes increasingly clear to me that she has a rigid attitude about

sorting things out for herself. So I ask her about this and she confirms it.]

Raniya: And I have to sort it out. Even the one issue with me is that I try to sort out everyone's problems in my surrounding because I feel that I'm responsible for them. Being elder, I'm responsible for them.

Windy: Yeah, but look at what you've done today. You've actually reached out to me. You're basically saying through your behaviour, 'Professor Dryden, give me some help.'

[*I point out to Raniya that by volunteering for the session with me that she is going against her rigid attitude and is seeking help from me.*]

Raniya: Yes.

Windy: And that's a first start. It's a great first start. Now, the point is, you prefer to sort things out on your own. That's fine, but you can do it flexibly or rigidly. You could say, 'Ideally, I'd like to help myself without help from others and, therefore, that's the way it's got to be. I can't go to anybody else,' or, 'I'd like to do it myself, but it doesn't always have to be that way. There might be exceptions to that and this is an exception.' So, without giving up your preference to do it on your own, you have a choice to be rigid or flexible about it.

[*I use again Windy's Review Assessment Procedure (WRAP) to help Raniya discriminate between making her preference rigid and keeping it flexible.*]

Raniya: Yes, I think I should be more flexible towards it and it's better to get help from someone else rather than managing everything on my own, because this is about helping me now, to a greater extent.

Windy: That's right. OK. So, why don't you summarise where we've got to so far, Raniya?

Raniya: I think the issue was that I have been compiling or thinking in multiple domains rather than focusing on what is the key issue, because I have this mindset that I can't go to anyone, without even realising that you in fact put forward, that I am discussing with you. I have come to you myself.

Windy: Yeah.

Raniya: That's the beginning. That's a good start that I should look at help and, rather than managing the issues with my son, it's better if I could take opinion from someone else who could guide me in a better way. And flexibility is a better solution.

Windy: That's right and you need to recognise that there are external resources in the environment that can help you.

Raniya: Yes.

Windy: There's a great phrase which I'm going to leave you with. It is this: only you can do it but you don't have to do it alone.

Raniya: Yes.

Windy: And you're operating on the idea, 'Only I can do it and I have to do alone.'

Raniya: Yes, that's true. That's my irrational belief: that I just have to do it.

Windy: Yeah, 'On my own.'

Raniya: On my own, yes. True.

Windy: But I think you've reached out to me, which is a fantastic start, and what I'm saying is capitalise on that. Still recognise that, yes, you're in charge, but you don't have to do it on your own and tell somebody upfront you don't want sympathy, you want help, and get rid of them if they give you sympathy without help because that's not for you. Alright?

Raniya: Yes, that's great.

Windy: So, let's take their questions and discussion.

[This session shows that something very useful can come from a brief 15 minute conversation when the focus emerges from the discussion rather than being stated by the person at the outset.]

10

Helping the Person to Deal with Anxiety about Seeing New Clients

Windy–Lara Interview on 26/04/21
Time: 19 minutes 6 secs

Windy: OK, Lara, what is your understanding of the purpose of our conversation today?

Lara: My understanding? … I've been following these sessions and I really like the questions you ask and they help to understand the issues in their core or to see the things that we don't really want to see or we cannot see for some reasons.

Windy: Yeah.

Lara: Yeah, and my issue is I've been training as an REBT therapist myself a couple of years ago or so and I've been practising with friends and acquaintances or friends of friends. I feel I would like to go further to a wider circle of people to work with, but I have this fear, I would say overwhelming fear. And I've been working with the other therapists and… I've made some progress but it's still there; it's not going.

Windy: What, your fear's not going?

Lara: Yeah, my fear is not going, the fear to start doing things. I have lots going on in my head.

Windy: I'm not sure what you're afraid of. What are you afraid of?

Lara: That's a good question. ... [*Long pause*] I'm afraid of starting working with others.

Windy: When you say 'others', you mean with clients?

Lara: Yeah, with clients, for example people who are not familiar, who I don't know.

Windy: OK. Let me just get the context, if I may. Do you mind if I ask you a few contextual questions?

[*Although I have limited time with the volunteer, I sometimes find it useful to understand the context of the problem so I ask Lara's permission to ask her a number of questions about this context.*]

Lara: Sure.

Windy: So, what training have you had in REBT and where did you get the training?

Lara: I got my training with the College of Cognitive-Behavioural Therapists and I've done my Advanced Integrative Diploma 1.

Windy: Right. So, how long have you been with them?

Lara: I got my diploma and accreditation with the National Counselling Society a couple of years ago.

Windy: OK. And have you been working with clients with REBT or not?

Lara: Yes, for these two years I've been working with clients. I usually have between two to five clients.

Windy: So, let me see if I get this straight: when you work with friends and friends of friends, you're not fearful.

Lara: No.

Windy: But, when you work with clients, you are fearful?

Lara: Yes. I'll give you an example. I'm registered on Psychology Today and the National Counselling Society and, when I receive calls from there, I'm already shaking and fearful there's somebody I don't know and am I going to be good enough, would I know what to do with them. It's a bit strange and possibly ridiculous.

Windy: But you don't get that with your friends and your friends of friends?

Lara: With friends, no. With friends of friends, a little bit, but I can overcome that, because, I don't know, somehow they are going through somebody; already they recommended me and they come with an idea of what to expect.

Windy: But, with your friends and, to some degree, with your friends of friends, do you have a greater sense that you're knowing what you're doing with these people?

Lara: Yes.

Windy: So, you know roughly what you're doing, but with the clients who you don't know, your immediate reaction is that you may not know what you're doing. Is that correct?

Lara: Yes.

[In asking these questions, I am getting a sense of Lara's main problem. I am now ready to ask her what she wants to achieve from our conversation.]

Windy: So, what's your goal in talking to me today? What would you like to achieve?

Lara: Ideally, I would like really to dissolve that fear.

Windy: To dissolve it into what?

Lara: To have rational understanding that there's nothing to be afraid of.

Windy: Well, but there might be something to be afraid of. You don't get over your fear by rubbing this thing three times and think, 'Oh, there's nothing to be afraid of,' because that's not what we're trying to do in REBT. We're trying to help you to deal with the adversity. And it sounds like, for you, the adversity is that somebody who you don't know comes to see you and that you may not know what to say or to do with them. That's what I'm hearing. Is that right?

[I am referring to rubbing Aladdin's Lamp, which I sometimes use as a prop in therapy. Here I make the important distinction between helping Lara to see that she has nothing to fear and helping here deal effectively with her adversity which, based on what she has told me, I put to her as a hypothesis.]

Lara: Yeah, that's right.

Windy: OK. So, let's suppose, for example, that, when a
              new client came to see you, you had a guarantee
              that you believed that you would know exactly
              what to do with them. Would you still be afraid
              under those conditions?

Lara: No.

*[I use this question a lot. I have named it 'Windy's Magic
Question'. What I am asking Lara is that if she had a
guarantee that the opposite of her adversity would occur (i.e.
that she knew for certain that she would know exactly how to
deal with new clients would she still be anxious. Lara confirms
that she wouldn't so I am strengthened in my view that her
adversity is 'not knowing what to do with a new client'.]*

Windy: So, again, you start with a very healthy preference
              which is this: 'When a client comes to see me, I
              would very much prefer to know what to do with
              them,' and then you tell me which attitude leads
              you to anxiety and which attitude would lead to
              what we would call healthy concern. So, the first
              attitude is: 'I very much want to know what to say
              and do with these clients, but I don't have to,' or,
              'I'd very much like to know what to do with these
              clients and therefore I absolutely have to know
              that.' Which attitude leads to your anxiety and
              which would lead to your healthy concern?

*[I follow this up with Windy's Review Assessment Procedure
(WRAP) to help Lara identify the attitude that underpins her
anxiety and the one that leads to concern.]*

Lara: Yeah, the second leads to anxiety.

Windy: That's right. Your first one would lead to healthy
              concern and you want to get rid of the adversity.
              You're saying, 'I want to get rid of the adversity.

There's nothing to be afraid of.' Well, there's nothing to be afraid of, but there might be something to be concerned about, because you're still relatively new as an REBT therapist. You might be very experienced with your friends and your friends of friends, but with clients you may not be that experienced and therefore the chances are that you may not know exactly what to say and, if you were concerned about that, then you would say, 'OK, I'll take that to supervision and figure that out.'

But let me ask you a question: which of those two attitudes I've outlined, both start off with the healthy desire: 'I very much would like to know what to do with clients when they come to see me,' which of those two attitudes is going to lead to anxiety and which attitude is going to lead to concern again? Let me just see if we can start off with that one again and then we can ask you other questions.

Lara: Yeah. The first one I don't have to; I would like to but I don't have to, yeah, it leads to concern, but the second one leads to anxiety. I'm allowing myself to go with it.

Windy: Well, you're allowing yourself to go with it instead of saying, 'Now, wait a minute, I'd better stop that and I'd better challenge it,' because you react to it with avoidance, don't you? You don't see these clients?

[Here I show that when Lara avoids seeing new clients she is depriving herself of the opportunity of examining and changing her rigid attitude to the flexible alternative.]

Lara: Yeah, avoidance and sabotage. I do everything.

Windy: How do you sabotage, by the way?

Lara: How do I sabotage? I've put a profile which I can see is possibly not attractive and I'm just like, 'Oh, it's there.'

Windy: Yeah. So, you're kind of fooling yourself that you're doing something to get a practice together, but you're also, at the same time, because of this fear, sabotaging yourself. Is that right?

[What Lara refers to as sabotage is really another form of avoidance. While convincing herself that she is facing her adversity, she sabotages herself by making her online professional profile unattractive, which results in new clients not contacting her.]

Lara: Yeah, that's right, and I'm not rushing to the answer the phone. I answer the phone, but I would delay that.

Windy: Yeah. Again, all these things are going to be keeping your anxiety alive rather than helping you to get yourself into a situation where you can actually deal with your underlying rigid attitude. Just because it's important to you and to the clients that you know what you're doing, how does it follow that therefore you have to know that?

Lara: … *[Pause]* I have to know what to do with the client?

Windy: Yeah. How does it follow that, because you want to know what to do and say, that therefore you have to know what to do and say?

Lara: It is very important to me.

Windy: That's not what I asked you. I didn't ask you how important it was. I know it's very important to you, but, just because it's very important to you, how does it follow that therefore you have to know what to do and say?

Lara: Oh yeah, of course there's no logic. It doesn't.

Windy: Right. And, incidentally, if such an attitude was true, you would just have to say, 'Because it's so important to me that I mustn't make mistakes, therefore I mustn't make mistakes,' and, if that were true, you couldn't make mistakes because your attitude would eradicate the possibility of you making mistakes. Does it?

[In the above sequence, I have asked Lara questions designed to help Lara examine the logic and validity of her rigid attitude.]

Lara: Yeah, I can see it now.

Windy: There's always the possibility of making mistakes in psychotherapy. Do you know what the biggest mistake that you can make as a therapist?

Lara: It's not the practice.

Windy: Believing that you mustn't make mistakes is one of the biggest mistakes that you can make as a therapist.

Lara: Yeah.

Windy: So, again, is this also a self-esteem issue? Let's suppose that you see a new client, the client comes and there you are, you're thinking, 'I don't know what to say and do,' would you be judging yourself in that situation?

[*Having helped Lara examine her rigid attitude, I decide to do some work on her accompanying self-devaluation attitude which I think she holds. So I first check to see if I am correct.*]

Lara: Yes.

Windy: What would you be judging yourself as?

Lara: ... I would be judging myself... thinking low of myself, like... I'm not really a therapist. That would be a bit harsh. I'm not really a therapist, like I don't still know what to do with a client. Maybe I shouldn't be doing this. Maybe I should still learn more.

Windy: Yeah. 'Maybe I need to learn more with my friends and my friends of friends.'

Lara: Yeah, and I'm doing lots of courses because I believe I need to.

[*Doing these courses serves to help Lara delay the time when she sees clients for REBT and feeds the myth that there is a course out there, which will magically transform her from a therapist who does not know what to do to a therapist who does. I refer to this below as going from a caterpillar therapist to a butterfly therapist.*]

Windy: Yeah. I think all of these things – which are friends and friends of friends and courses – are feeding into the problem, because I think underneath that you've got the idea, 'If I see the friends and the friends of friends and if I do all of these courses, then I will reach the stage of knowing what to do with these clients.'

Lara: Yes, and I'll be a grown therapist and confident.

Windy: That's right. 'I'll go from being a caterpillar therapist to a butterfly therapist overnight.' And then you'll say, 'Oh no, wait a minute, I don't feel it, because there's a course out there which, if I take, I will immediately shed my skin and start flying through the therapeutic space knowing exactly what to say and where to say it and how to say it.'

Lara: Yes, that's exactly. Thank you.

Windy: Instead, I would say that you need to clear the ground and really take the risk and start seeing clients and start really getting yourself into this situation which says, 'Look, of course I don't want to make mistakes and of course I would like to know what to say, it's very important, but, if I don't demand that of myself, if I allow myself not to know what to say and take that to supervision, then I will build up my confidence as a therapist,' because you're not going to go from being a caterpillar therapist to a butterfly therapist overnight. So, I would say no more friends of friends, rush to the phone when it rings, get them in and really work on helping yourself to give up these rigid, self-rejecting attitudes that you have and really work on showing yourself – the idea that, when you start seeing clients that you have to know what to say and what to do right from the start is based on some kind of myth: the Lara myth of REBT, which is the myth of, when you start seeing clients, you immediately know what to say and do.

[Here I outline what Lara needs to do to address her problem. This is based on the principle that the best way to deal with her

anxiety is to face the adversity and do so while developing her flexible and unconditional self-acceptance attitudes.]

Lara:　I had the impression that this is what a good therapist is: immediately knowing what to do.

Windy:　In which case why would they need supervision? Why would they need training and all that? A good therapist becomes a good therapist because, 1) they allow themselves the possibility of not knowing what to say, not knowing what to do; accept themselves for it; take it to supervision, learn from it and build up and become confident that way, as opposed to going in there with immediate confidence, because that's what you want to do. You want to immediately start to be confident. And you're perpetuating the problem with all of these: the more you do the friends and the friends of friends, you think you're helping yourself, but you're perpetuating the problem. So, redo the psychology profile today and make yourself very attractive for clients to contact you. Get them in and really get a good supervisor and make those tapes, because I think the best way of actually learning to be a good REBT therapist is having your tapes supervised. Not just talking about what you did, having your tapes supervised.

Let's hear from your perspective what we've covered today and what you're going to take away from today.

Lara:　It was interesting to discover this demand. It was very interesting from the perspective of I believe I know it and I do tell people, even myself, that we learn from mistakes, but, in a way, I wasn't really aware that I have this demand. I couldn't see it in myself that I have this demand not to make mistakes. It has beautifully surfaced in this session that I have a very strong, rigid demand and, therefore, I sabotage working with a wider circle of people or with clients who are not familiar. It brings relief and that shadow of fear has dissipated for me. It's taking responsibility now and moving forward.

Windy: Either that or you set up a practice which just involves you seeing friends and friends of friends. 'In my practice, I don't see anybody that I don't know.'

[Here I use humour to underscore the point.]

Lara: Yes, and I understand and what I'm taking as well, it's OK to make mistakes; it's OK not to know as a therapist, taking it to supervision, learning from there, and this is how I would grow as a therapist.

Windy: And I think you're also making another fundamental error in your thinking.

Lara: Already.

Windy: I think you're placing friends and friends of friends in a completely and utterly different category than clients, whereas I see all of them as being human. You almost see them as different species.

[This is another way in which Lara perpetuates her anxiety by seeing her friends as very different from new clients.]

Lara: Yeah.

Windy: 'There's this client species over here. Nothing to do with these friends and friends of friends species over here. They're from a different planet.'

Lara: That's exactly how I see it. Thank you.

Windy: Whereas really aren't they linked by their
               humanity? The other thing you can do to help
               yourself is to say, 'Look, clients are humans.
               They're not from a different planet, and therefore I
               can use some of the skills that I have learnt with
               friends and friends of friends and I can use them
               here, and it might be different because I don't
               know them and that's the purpose of the
               supervision.' So, that's the other thing I would just
               urge you to do: to recognise that your clients are
               human as well as your friends and your friends of
               friends. OK?

Lara: Yes, OK. Thank you.

Windy: OK, let's see what the group's got to say.

11

Helping the Person to Bear Her Anxiety Symptoms

Windy–Raj Interview on 08/03/21
Time: 15 minutes 36 secs

Windy: What's your understanding of the purpose of our conversation today?

Raj: Hopefully, you'll be able to help me sort my anxiety issues.

Windy: And what are you anxious about?

Raj: Actually, I'll tell you, say a bit about my background. I used to work with the airlines and I used to travel a lot, and it's been around 16 years now that I've stopped working because I had a child and then my father-in-law used to live with me, who was quite old – he just passed away last year at the age of 93. So, what I suffer from is anxiety. I have a problem staying alone, doing anything alone, going to places alone, mainly driving anywhere alone, like even if I have to go to the supermarket, I'd always tell my husband or my daughter, who's 13, to come with me.

Windy: Is there some explanation that you have for that? Did something happen to you at some point?

Raj: No, not really. I think what happened was, the year
              during the Olympics I had people come and stay
              with me and just before that I had a friend of mine
              who was detected with bipolar, and I think that
              was also the first time had met somebody who was
              bipolar and I didn't know she was bipolar. She had
              just had a baby and she called me and she said,
              'Let's meet at the pub.' So, I said, 'OK, let's go
              and meet at the pub.' And, when I went to the pub,
              there was a nurse with her and the nurse told me,
              'You need to drop her back to the hospital,' and I
              was like, 'Hospital? Why hospital?' and she said,
              'You need to drop her to the Bethlehem
              Psychiatric Hospital,' which is in West Wickham.
              And I said, 'OK,' and then my friend had this very
              kind of strange behaviour and I think that's when I
              first got my panic attack because I didn't know
              what she was doing, because she had ordered
              everything on the menu and a lot of strange
              behaviour which was not very common.

Windy: OK, that was your first introduction to the fact that
              you were sitting with a person with somewhat
              unpredictable behaviour.

Raj: Mental health. Yes, unpredictable behaviour. So, I
              went and dropped her to the hospital with another
              friend of hers and both of us had our first minor
              panic attack, I would say, maybe had shortness of
              breath. And then I came home, I called my
              husband and I still had heavy breathing. And this
              happened in 2012 and that was the same time
              when my friends had come from India for the
              Olympics, and I think it was the stress that I
              couldn't handle. There was one morning I just
              couldn't come down and face them. I just couldn't
              handle the stress of what had just happened a few
              days earlier and this.

Windy: Right, OK. So, let's say that that contributed to the problem. Now, before that experience, were you OK being on your own?

Raj: 100% OK. 100%.

Windy: OK, alright. So, we could say that that event contributed to your problem, not caused it because, if we had 100 people in that situation, not all of them would've had a panic attack and certainly not all of them would've developed an ongoing fear of being on their own. But let's have a look at now, OK?

[*This is an important point stemming from REBT theory. Events like the one mentioned by Raj contribute to people's problems, they do not cause them.*]

Raj: Yeah.

Windy: How does this problem affect you now?

Raj: I think now I have gotten over the experience of meeting somebody with the same disorder, because I have another friend of mine who's having the same issue and it's one of my closest school friends, and I'm very comfortable when I'm talking with her. But I think back then it was just a major shock, because I wasn't aware of it.

Windy: I'm still interested in how that's a problem for you now going forward.

Raj: That is what I can't link.

Windy: Are you able to go out on your own now?

Raj: With a lot of difficulty. So, I do work in a school.

Windy: Would you like to go out on your own now?

Raj: Yes, I want to go back to travelling alone.

Windy: So, let's help you to do that, alright?

Raj: Yes.

[Once I have helped Raj to specify a goal, I ask her below to select an imminent example of her problem. This will help us both understand the factors that explain her problem and provide a setting where she can tackle this problem.]

Windy: OK. Now, let's make it really imminent. What would you like to do in the next 24 hours that would give you a sign that you'd begun to deal with this problem, that you would be fearful of doing? What real thing could you do?

Raj: I think I would like to probably try and do things that make me anxious, like shopping, going to the supermarket and just basic.

Windy: OK. So, where's the supermarket to you?

Raj: It would be maybe around 10 minutes away from me.

Windy: Ten minutes walking?

Raj: I would say a drive, because I don't want to go to the nearest supermarket because there's never any parking. You never get a slot there. So, I would like to drive.

Windy: But, if you walk there, you don't need to park, do you? But, anyway, so, you want to drive to the supermarket. OK, right.

Raj: Yes, because I have an issue driving and going alone as well.

Windy: OK. So, the first thing is that you're anxious about driving on your own.

Raj: Yes.

Windy: Would you be anxious if you were driving and somebody was sitting next to you?

Raj: I'm completely fine. So, if I have my husband or my daughter, I'm completely fine.

Windy: OK. You see, the two components of your anxiety are: 1) what you predict is going to happen, in other words the threat; and, 2) your capacity for dealing with the threat.

Raj: Yes.

Windy: Now, which do you think is a major feature of your anxiety: the fact that a threat might occur or your perceived ability to deal with the threat?

Raj: To deal with it.

Windy: So, what do you think could happen if you drove from home to the supermarket that you would be anxious about because, largely, that you wouldn't be able to deal with it?

Raj: I think getting to the point where I'm so nervous, where I just can't move.

Windy: Right. So, you're anxious about your anxiety.

Raj: Yes.

Windy: OK. Now, what is it about your anxiety that you're anxious about?

[I use the concept of anxiety about anxiety to help Raj to identify what she is most anxious about at C in the ABC framework with respect to her anxiety at A.]

Raj: … I think more bodily symptoms is what affects me.

Windy: OK, what aspects of the bodily symptoms are you most anxious about?

Raj: Like I think what annoys me or frustrates me is that, every time I get anxious, even though I tell my mind it is the way I'm thinking, I need to still do it, my legs feel numb and cold.

Windy: Fine, and then how do you react to your legs going cold? What's your reaction to that?

Raj: I think I try to distract myself every time I have these symptoms.

Windy: But, if you didn't distract yourself, what would be your reaction to it?

Raj: … My reaction to that would be…, no, I think I generally try to distract myself.

Windy: I know you do, but, if you didn't, what would your reaction be?

Raj: I would just let it go, let it take its course, maybe.

Windy: So, why don't you do that?

Raj: OK. OK.

Windy: Because I'm hearing that either you're saying to yourself, 'If my legs go numb, that would be terrible and, therefore, I have to distract myself,' or, 'If my legs go numb, it would be uncomfortable but not terrible.' Now, which do you think you honestly do believe at that time that, if your legs go numb, that would be terrible and you couldn't bear it or that it would be unpleasant, it would be a struggle to put up with, but you could bear it?

Raj: I think struggle to put up with it but could bear it.

Windy: But then why distract yourself from that, because, if you didn't distract yourself from it and said, 'Look, OK, I'm going out, my legs are going to go numb, I'm going to have other bodily symptoms, I don't like that but I'm going to tolerate it, I'm going to put up with it and that's the way forward,' wouldn't you solve your problem after a while?

[*Here I am trying to show Raj that if she did hold a bearability attitude towards her legs going cold or numb then she would not distract herself.*]

Raj: Yes, but I think what happens is, when I do let it takes its course, I think what happens is, because it happens so regularly, I just think I can't take it anymore.

Windy: Exactly, and it's the 'I can't take it anymore' that is the thing. Now, do you have any kids?

[*So Raj holds an unbearability attitude about the regularity of her bodily symptoms.*]

Raj: Yes, I have a daughter.

Windy: OK. So, if we said at that point, 'OK, you can't take it anymore, we'll remove the problem for you, but, unfortunately, we're taking your child away and you'll never see her again,' would you say, 'OK, that's a good deal'?

Raj: No. No.

Windy: Why not?

Raj: No.

Windy: So, why wouldn't you do that?

Raj: … No, because she's a part of me.

Windy: Yeah, but you're a part of you. That's very interesting. You said, 'I'm prepared to tolerate it for my daughter who's a part of me, but I'm not prepared to tolerate it for me, who's also a part of me.' Now, what would happen if you then said, 'Look, no matter how uncomfortable it is, I'm just going to put up with it and go forward. I'm not going to distract myself. I'm just going to make my goal the supermarket and I'm just going to let it go,' and, when you say to yourself, 'I can't stand it anymore,' you say, 'Yes, I can, because I'd stand it to save my child, of course I would. So, I'm going to stand it for my mental health,' unless you don't think you're worth it, Raj?

[*What I am doing here is showing Raj that there would be conditions where she would choose to bear her bodily symptoms –to preserve the safety of her daughter. Thus, she can bear these symptoms. Given that, if she chose to bear her symptoms for the benefit for her own mental health and did so consistently then she would solve her problem.*]

Raj: Yeah.

Windy: Do, you think you're worth doing it for?

Raj: Yes. Yes.

Windy: Right, because I hear you saying, 'Of course I'd do it for my child, she's worth doing it for because she's part of me,' but then you've got to take the same attitude towards yourself, right?

Raj: Towards myself, yeah. I think because of this I've lost my self-confidence.

Windy: Well, that's true, but let's take it one step at a time. Your first stance is to develop an attitude of bearability: 'I am going to bear the bodily symptoms. They are uncomfortable, they are painful, I don't need to distract myself from them. I can go forward even though they're there and, if I tell myself I can't bear it, I'm going to tell myself, no, I can bear it because I would bear it for my dear child and I'll bear it for my dear self.' Now, if you practised that philosophy going forward, what difference would that make to you, Raj?

Raj: I think, slowly and gradually, I'll get used to it.

Windy: If you did it every day, if you resolved to do something like that every day and don't duck out of it because of distraction or because you think you can't bear it, if you really committed yourself to it, to do something like that for the next 30 days, then you can come back here in a month's time and tell us how you're getting on and we'll take you to the next stage.'

Raj: OK, great, yes.

Windy: Alright?

Raj: Yes.

Windy: OK, so, what have you learnt today?

Raj: That I need to actually not distract myself and give myself a goal and accept all the feelings that I'm having.

[A good succinct summary by Raj.]

Windy: Yeah, because the other thing that initially was the problem was that you didn't know anything about this person's problem and it was a bit of a shock to you and then you had the reactions and then you got focused on your reactions.

Raj: Yes, because before that I'd never known what a panic attack was. I'd never had symptoms of being nervous, because my job profile was very stressful with the airlines because I took care of ambassadors, diplomats, prime ministers who travelled with the airlines, never had any anxiety, nothing. And I think the first time I felt the bodily symptoms, maybe I'm thinking now that I'm linking everything to my bodily symptoms; I'm focusing more on my bodily symptoms.

Windy: That's right. That's what Albert Ellis called 'anxiety about anxiety', one of the first people to call it that and, because you're always going to have a body and you experience your anxiety mainly through your bodily symptoms – people experience their anxiety in very different ways – you then focus on your body, you tell yourself, 'I can't bear it. I have to distract myself from it or I have to avoid situations where I might feel this way,' and then you actually maintain the problem.

Raj: Yes.

Windy: But, if you really recognise that it is going to be uncomfortable, it's not great, but it's bearable and you're really prepared to bear it as you would be if you were to save your life of your child, you do something every day, come back in a month and we'll see how you go, OK?

[*This is my summary for Raj which I could have omitted but reinforces her own summary.*]

Raj: OK, I'm going to do that.

Windy: Good.

Raj: Thank you.

12

Helping the Person to Deal with Her Anger Towards Her Brother

Windy–Elsie Interview on 08/02/21
Time: 18 minutes 49 secs

Windy: What's your understanding of the purpose of our conversation today?

Elsie: That you would hopefully talk some sense into me and try and make my bad situation not worse.

Windy: Wow, that's a lot of power for me, isn't it? Who needs my lamp when you've got Dryden? I'll tell you what, how about if I help you to talk some sense into yourself and help you to make your bad situation rather better? How's that? Is that good compromise since I don't have the magic? Listen, if I had the magic, I'd do it for you, but then I wouldn't need to talk to you; I'd just be doing it.

[At the outset I am clear with Elsie what I can do and what I can't do.]

Elsie: OK.

Windy: Right, so what's the problem?

Elsie: So, my problem is I have probably anger, anxiety and hurt, but mainly anger is the one I want to work on.

148

Windy: OK, anger at what?

Elsie: And it's towards a sibling I have where I'm damning them for the situation they've got themselves into.

Windy: And what is that situation that they've got themselves into?

Elsie: So, I have a sibling who has got multiple addictions.

Windy: Male or female?

Elsie: A brother, so a male sibling who drinks, smokes, gambles, food. Anyway, he ended up unable to look after himself and got kicked out by his wife, lost his job, all sorts. Therefore, also this has caused him to have health problems and financial problems and he's also got personal hygiene problems, various things, lack of social interactions, he's got no friends, no connections. And then I think my demand is people shouldn't be a burden to others. So, I think then I've got this demand thing where I'm thinking, 'Your problems are all self-inflicted. You shouldn't be a burden. You shouldn't be dependent on others.'

[*These latter statements indicate that Elsie's anger is unhealthy.*]

Windy: Who's he a burden on?

Elsie: Well, because he's unable to deal with a lot of his problems, he ended up on the streets, in fact. So, I have multiple siblings and we all join in and sort the problems out. There are lots of them that occur all the time.

Windy: Right. So, he lives on the streets at the moment?

Elsie: No, we've kind of taken him, sorted him out, but it's just one problem after another has happened – bad teeth, bad eyes.

Windy: So, where's he living now?

Elsie: He's living with my mother at the moment.

Windy: OK. And you're angry with him because he's a burden on whom?

Elsie: Yeah, a burden on me.

Windy: How's he a burden on you?

[*Here I am endeavouring to understand the context before intervening.*]

Elsie: Because I'm constantly having to sort out his problems for him.

Windy: Constantly having to or constantly choosing to?

Elsie: Constantly choosing to, I suppose. We've divvied all the problems up between us.

Windy: Right, but it's still a choice, isn't it? It's still a choice.

Elsie: Yeah, I could say, 'I'm not doing any of it.'

Windy: Yeah, you could say that. Why don't you say that?

Elsie: Because I feel a sense of responsibility towards it.

Windy: A responsibility to do what?

Elsie: A responsibility to wave a magic wand and sort them all out; be a fixit person.

Windy: Yeah, that'd be nice, but think about it clearly: a responsibility to do what?

Elsie: A responsibility to not make the situations he's got into even worse.

Windy: Right. So, you're prepared to do a certain level of things and that's your choice and then what's his responsibility in response to your responsibility?

Elsie: He does some of them as well, but he needs coaching to do them, otherwise he will do avoidance tactics.

Windy: And you provide the coaching or what?

Elsie: Yeah. So, for him to go online to sort out a financial problem, he won't do it unless I sit with him.

Windy: Right, OK, and you're prepared to sit with him, are you?

Elsie: Yeah, but, whilst I'm sitting with him, I'm feeling angry.

Windy: Because you're demanding what?

[*As Elsie relates this event she mentions the point at which she is experiencing anger. I respond by asking her what she is demanding. This is a theoretically driven question since in REBT we argue that unhealthy anger is based on a demand.*]

Elsie: Because I've got the demand that he shouldn't have gotten into this mess in the first place.

Windy: Well, I would put the opposite argument: I think
               he should've gotten into this mess in the first
               place. Now, we both can't be right, can we,
               because you're demanding that he shouldn't and
               I'm saying that he should. Now, there's only one
               way of determining who's right and that's reality.
               So, whose side is reality on: your side or my side?

*[Here I invite Elsie to compare her absolute should with my
empirical should and to see whose side reality is on hers or
mine.]*

Elsie: Your side.

Windy: Right, OK. So, aren't you demanding that reality
               not be reality?

Elsie: Yeah. So, I'm demanding that people live this
               plain-sailing life where nothing happens.

*[I don't want Elsie to go to the general case so below I
encourage her to keep the focus on her brother.]*

Windy: Don't worry about people. Just concentrate on
               your brother. You're demanding that your brother
               should not have gotten himself into this position in
               the first place and I'm saying he should have done
               that, not that it's a good thing, that I'm
               recommending it. I'm using what we call in REBT
               the empirical should. Sadly and regretfully and
               somewhat tragically all the conditions are in place
               for him to end up exactly where he is. Now, by
               demanding that this absolutely shouldn't have
               happened to him, what's the purpose of that
               demand, Elsie? When you're demanding that,
               what's the purpose of your demand?

Elsie: I suppose I'm trying to change history.

Windy: That's right. You're trying to go back and change history. Listen, I said this to Maggie with her magic cookie:[6] if you find a way to change history, please email me, let me be the first person to benefit from Elsie's method of rewriting history. Is that a deal?

Elsie: Yeah.

Windy: Because the chances of you rewriting history are what?

Elsie: Zero.

Windy: Well, 0.1. We can't say absolutely, but I wouldn't put any money on it. Whereas I'm saying, look, all the conditions are right for it to happen and it happened and then going forward you're going to have to ask yourself the question, 'What am I prepared to do for my brother allowing for the fact, sadly, that he may do nothing for himself?'

[Once Elsie has adopted the empirical should rather than her rigid should she can then ask herself the question I posed above.]

Elsie: … *[Long pause]*

Windy: What are you going to do for him allowing for the fact that he may do nothing for himself?

Elsie: Well, I would like to keep on sorting the problems out so that I can stop the future becoming worse.

Windy: Well, try to, because you're not going to be there 24/7, are you?

---

[6] Maggie was the previous volunteer.

Elsie: But what I don't want to do is with the bad thoughts towards him.

Windy: Right. So, you can go in there and say to yourself, 'I am choosing to do this for my brother because he's my brother and I love him' – is that right, you love him?

Elsie: …

Windy: Love-ish – 'I love him ish.' Right, OK. 'I care about him,' then. Is that right?

Elsie: Yeah.

Windy: 'I'm prepared to do this for my brother because I care about him and I'm doing it hoping that it will have an effect, but it doesn't have to, because I'm doing this because I don't want it to be worse.' Now, how about if you went in with that philosophy?

[Here I have taken elements of what we have already discussed and suggested a course of action based on a flexible attitude.]

Elsie: Yeah, that's a much softer, calmer, rational one.

Windy: Yeah. Have you got any objections to that philosophy? I know you still want to go back and change the past and that would be great, but do you have any objections to that or doubts or reservations to that philosophy going forward?

Elsie: No, I like that. What I'd like to also be able to do, though, is tolerate his unhygienic-ness.

Windy: OK. Tolerate to what extent?

Elsie: Well, at the moment I turn up and say, 'Can you go and have a shower?'

Windy: Yeah.

Elsie: 'Can you put on some new clothes?'

Windy: And what does he do? Does he do that?

Elsie: Yeah, he does do that, but I don't want to be having to say it.

Windy: What would you rather happen then?

Elsie: Well, I'd rather tolerate him coming with me in the state he's in and me not worrying about it.

Windy: OK, let's see first of all what you're going to tolerate. What is it that you want to tolerate? The smells?

Elsie: Yeah, I want to tolerate the smell, perhaps the worry of the thoughts of others towards us.

Windy: OK. Let's take it one stage at a time. You want to tolerate the smell – the smell of what?

Elsie: Well, because there's a smell of smoke, just a damp, dark smell of despair.

Windy: I thought you were going to say vomit, urine and shit.

Elsie: There is urine sometimes.

Windy: There is urine, OK. How would you tolerate it? Let's see how you would tolerate it. Let's suppose you decided to do that, what discomfort tolerance

attitude could you develop towards that? Let's see
if you could figure that out?

Elsie: Well, if I'm in a confined space, I open the
window.

Windy: Fine. Well, every little helps.

Elsie: But I could do the: I would prefer him not to be
smelling, but he doesn't absolutely have to.

Windy: 'And I find it unpleasant.'

Elsie: Yeah, but it's not the end of the world.

Windy: 'But I can tolerate it,' and it's worth tolerating?

Elsie: Yeah, because I don't want to be a nag.

[*Here with prompting, Elise articulates flexible and non-
awfulising attitudes towards the adversity of her brother's
unpleasant odour. I add the discomfort tolerance attitude[7] for
good measure.*]

Windy: OK. You see, the components of discomfort
tolerance are, 1) 'It's difficult tolerating it' – it's
what I call the struggle component – 'but I can
tolerate it,' 'It's worth it to me to tolerate it,' 'I'm
willing to tolerate it because I don't want to be a
nag,' and, 'I'm going to tolerate it,' with a little
help occasionally from an opened window. Do you
think you can do that going forward?

[*Here I specify the five components of a discomfort tolerance
or bearability attitude.*]

---

[7] I now refer to a discomfort tolerance attitude as a bearability attitude
and a discomfort intolerance attitude as an unbearability attitude.

Elsie: Yes, I'll practise that. I'll write that down and practise that.

Windy: Let's have a look at the other thing which is the tolerance of other people's views. What thoughts do they have, do you think?

[*We have time to deal with this issue although there is a question whether I am covering too much ground in this session. I could have asked Elsie for her opinion on this issue rather than take a unilateral position. In single-session work, there is a fine line between not doing enough and doing too much in a session.*]

Elsie: Yeah, I would worry that they would think, 'Look at those scumbags walking along.'

Windy: Well, are you scumbags?

Elsie: … Potentially, because often the only way I can get him out is if we go litter-picking.

Windy: Yeah, but, as a human being, are you a scumbag? Is a human being a scumbag?

Elsie: … No. I suppose no, and neither is he.

Windy: Right. So, you could actually say, 'Look, when we go out, whoever they are, these people are going to think, 'Oh, look at those scumbags,' they're either right about us – we are scumbags, or they're wrong about us – we're fallible human beings and we can accept ourselves even though they may not accept us.' Now, what would happen if you practised that attitude?

[*In this intervention, I am showing Elsie that she is in charge of how she defines herself and her brother and that she can uphold healthy self-definitions even in the face of unhealthy definitions of them by other people.*]

Elsie: That would be perfect, because then I wouldn't be concerned about others' opinions.

Windy: Well, you'd still be concerned about it because your preference is that you don't want them to think that way about you. So, we want you to be concerned about it, but we don't want you to be worried, because worried is saying, 'Wouldn't it be terrible if they thought we were scumbags? If we thought we were scumbags, they're right.' Well, they're wrong and it's hardly the end of the world, because you pass by and that's it. And you're doing that because you don't want to be a nag and also show your brother what? By going out with him, what are you showing him?

[*Here I make the point that Elsie would still be concerned about the opinion of others because she has a preference in this regard. I also make the point that she is trying to show her brother something by accompanying him outside.*]

Elsie: That he's got a connection with somebody.

Windy: That's right. That he can actually still connect with another human being, which I think is important for him. Where I live there's a person who lives on the streets and what I do is I do make sure that every time I pass him I mention his name, because I do want him to have even a small human connection, and I think what you're doing is really saying that, 'You may have got yourself into this state and I really wish I could turn back the clocks of time and stop it, but I can't and you are there because of your own responsibilities, etc., etc., and this is what I'm prepared to do to really help you and I'm prepared to tolerate the slings and fortunes of other people's views and also I'm prepared to tolerate your smell from time to time, but your my brother and this is what I'm going to do for you.' That's what I'm hearing that you could do.

[Throughout the session, I am not only working to help Elsie develop a set of flexible and non-extreme attitudes towards her brother and related issues, but I am showing her that she can set boundaries concerning what she is prepared to do to help him and what she is not prepared to do.]

Elsie: Yes.

Windy: Now, if you practised those philosophies, what difference would it make to you?

Elsie: Yeah, I would hopefully not have the anger and the anxiety.

Windy: That's right. If you started to make yourself angry, you could ask yourself, 'Am I once again demanding that he absolutely shouldn't have gotten himself into this position in the first place? And, if I do,' what are you going to tell yourself?

[I remind Elsie that she can use her anger quickly to detect her underlying demand and respond to it.]

Elsie: That... he... absolutely... doesn't – reverse it.

Windy: Yeah, that sadly and regretfully he should have got himself into this place because he did.

Elsie: Because he's a fallible human, yeah.

Windy: That's right. 'He's a fallible human being and reality was such that he made the choices that he made, got the consequences that he got and I really wish it wasn't like that. It would be nice if I could turn back the hands of the time, but sadly I can't and nor do I have to.'

Elsie: And, hopefully, if I can work on that, then I wouldn't also project around myself or other people that, 'You shouldn't be a burden, you shouldn't have gotten in that mess.'

Windy: That's right.

Elsie: Being judgemental that way.

Windy: That's right and that, 'He has gotten himself into that situation, he has gotten himself into that mess and I'm going to figure out just what I'm going to do and not do, what my limits are with him, but I'm going to figure out what I'm going to do and do it and I'm going to figure out what I'm not going to do and I'm not going to do.' And, therefore, he doesn't become a burden because you're making choices.

Elsie: Yeah. Fortunately, my burden is shared, but I would like to take the word 'burden' out of the whole scenario: that it's not a burden.

Windy: Fine, OK. Don't forget, although the 'burden' is shared, you could share around this rational philosophy so that everybody who's helping him is rational and you can teach them.

Elsie: ... Yes, if they'll listen to me.

Windy: Well, that's another thing, isn't it? One can bring words to a person's ears, but we can't guarantee that their brain is going to process it in the way that we'd like them to process it.

Elsie: That was very helpful and I did feel that got my goal of you talking some sense into me and me talking some sense into me.

Windy: That's right. At least it was a joint effort. Alright, thanks a lot. Let's see if there are any questions.

13

Helping the Person to Address Her Anxiety about Implementing REBT

Windy–Cora: Interview on 03/11/20
Time: 20 minutes 20 secs

Windy: Hi, Cora. Nice of you to join us.

Cora: Hi.

Windy: What's your understanding of the purpose of our session this evening?

Cora: My understanding is that we can talk about a problem that I have and you will cure me.

[*This is said humorously by Cora.*]

Windy: Well, no pressure there then, is there?

Cora: That was promising.

Windy: So, what are you doing while I'm curing you? Are you an active participant or are you just lying back and being cured?

[*Cora's humorous remark gives me an opportunity to invite her to be an active participant in the conversation that we are going to have.*]

Cora: Well, I guess I am an active participant, yes.

Windy: OK, that's good. So, if at the end of our session you walked away satisfied with what we discussed, what would you walk away with?

Cora: Maybe feeling a little bit more confident and just having maybe some tools to deal with some of my anxieties or insecurities that I have.

[*While asking for a session goal is a common question in single-session work, it often yields rather vague answers such as that given by Cora. Confidence and 'tools' are often mentioned in this regard by volunteers.*]

Windy: Yeah. Are you facing right now in your life one particular anxiety or insecurity that you'd like to focus on this evening?

Cora: Yeah. I was hoping we can focus on what I'm experiencing in sessions when I see my own clients. I just trained in REBT in the primary in September, so I'm trying to apply this very new model in my sessions. And I just find myself spinning my head a lot while I'm in session and just having a hard time being present because I'm so anxious about… not doing the right thing or doing anything effective at all. So, I just find myself being… just so nervous that I sometimes even miss things.

Windy: Sure. Have you had training in any other approach before or are you new to the whole field of counselling and therapy?

Cora: Well, I've had some training. I haven't had extensive continuous training. I've had like days of training where I'd just learn about an approach, but I haven't had where I would just be consistently trained. I have had supervision. So, I feel like I have general counselling skills. I think I'm definitely good with following a client-driven approach, but, as I am trying to be more active directive, that's where I just find my anxiety just really kicks in.

Windy: OK. And have you ever had the experience of learning anything in life and starting very anxious and unconfident and then ending up becoming more confident and dealing with your anxiety? Have you had that experience in life?

[*Here I am adopting single-session thinking which encourages me to help the person identify a similar situation where she began with the same or similar problem and then helped herself. If the person mentions they have had such an experience I can use helpful elements in the ensuing conversation.*]

Cora: I have, yeah.

Windy: Yeah? In what area that is probably most similar to the skills that we're talking about here?

Cora: ... Well,... [*pause*] I mean, I trained, for example, in motivational interviewing, and I feel like I'm confident – I'm not an expert, but I'm OK for my purposes.

Windy: And how did you feel when you were starting off with motivational interviewing?

Cora: Well, I felt pretty lost as well.

Windy: OK. So, how did you get from being lost and anxious with motivational interviewing to being more confident? How did you manage that?

Cora: I guess just... keep practising it in session and just really focusing on one skill at a time. I think maybe, as I'm speaking about this, that's what I'm trying to absorb the whole model and I've got a bunch of your books and I'm just really overwhelmed. So, I think I was focusing more on one thing at a time when I was doing motivational interviewing.

Windy: And was that helpful to you?

Cora: Yes. I mean, it's good to have the full picture, but, when I was trying to actually do it and apply it,... when I think about all of the elements, I just get lost. So, yeah.

Windy: Is this the motivational interviewing or the REBT?

Cora: Well, I guess it's both, but, with the motivational interviewing, I felt like I was able, maybe it was a little bit easier for me, just more natural, and I just sort of said, 'OK, I'll just practise this one skill and I'm just going to do this.'

Windy: Right. So, you focused on one skill. It was more synchronous with the way you work anyway. So, what would happen if you focused on one skill at a time while learning to develop as an REBT practitioner? What do you think would happen if you allowed yourself to do that?

[I wished I had asked and what do you think would happen with your anxiety if you allowed yourself to focus on one skill at a time. However, Cora will soon reveal her rigid attitudes that underpin her anxiety.]

Cora: I think maybe it would be just like not as effective. Maybe that's what I think. It's just I'm further along in my journey as a therapist and I just have maybe the expectation of myself that I should be able to grasp more of a big picture and being able to flexibly navigate the session.

Windy: So, just go over to me those two 'shoulds'? What were those two 'shoulds'?

Cora: So, I should be more flexible, so I should have more skills as a therapist.

Windy: And is that the way do you think you're thinking while you're trying to do REBT in session?

Cora: ... [*Pause*] Well, I think my thinking is more like, 'Oh gosh, what do I do next?' and just anxious thinking.

[*This shows clearly that while rigid attitudes are at the core of a person's anxiety, the person is likely to be more aware of anxious thoughts at the surface of their thinking – as is the case with Elsie.*]

Windy: And what do you think you're demanding at that point when you're wondering about what to do?

[*The REBT response is to invite the person to look for the demands that underpin such thinking.*]

Cora: I'm demanding that I'm already proficient in it while I'm just starting out.

Windy: Right, exactly. Now, when you stand back and think about that, what do you think?

Cora: Yeah, of course, I mean that makes sense to me that that makes me anxious, that thinking. It's exactly the part of the model that I'm trying to...

Windy: Right. Well, let's just help you to focus tonight on you being both your own REBT therapist and your own REBT client, so we can see what effectiveness can come out of really focusing on one skill at a time. How would you dispute that? There's Cora, the client, over here saying, 'Oh, I've got to be able to do it,' and there's Cora, the therapist. How are you going to help Cora, the client?

[Working with different parts can be a very useful way of helping the person in single-session work.]

Cora: Well, first of all I would probably see well is it really helpful to be focusing so much on what you should be doing instead of just giving yourself a break and just having more helpful thinking.

Windy: OK, right. So, you've focused on really identifying the should and then starting to question it in terms of the helpfulness. Right.

Cora: Yeah.

Windy: And what do you think that part of you that's the client is going to say, the part of you that's anxious? What are you going to say in response?

Cora: Well, of course it's not helpful, but that's just there. I want to be a good therapist, I want to have good results with clients, I want to help my clients.

Windy: Alright. So, Cora, the client, comes back and says, 'Yeah, but I want to help my clients,' right? So, Cora, the therapist, hears that and says what?

Cora: … Sure, yeah, I mean, of course, that's why you're a therapist. At the same time, I could try to think about a friend…

Windy: OK, yeah.

Cora: …who is going through the same thing and what would you think about or what would you suggest the friend does? And, yeah, I mean, if I think about my therapist friends, I… would say we always have to start somewhere and we're nervous and that's OK. … [*Long pause*] Yeah. I think that's a hard one for me because I'm in my own way, somewhat.

Windy: In what way are you in your own way?

Cora: Like I guess I just don't want to let go of that demand.

Windy: So, you don't want to let go of that demand because?

Cora: … [*Pause*] Yeah, because what would it leave me with? Maybe… I guess, so, instead of demanding to be a proficient, effective therapist, I would just have to accept that I am not.

Windy: Well, I have a different perspective, if you're interested?

[*Cora shows in the above responses that she is reluctant to let go of her demand that she has to be an effective, proficient therapist because doing so means to her acknowledging that she is not such a therapist. Before I respond to this, I ask Cora if she is interested in my perspective on the issue. Once a person has said 'yes' to such a question, doing so will increase the chances that they will listen to me with an open mind.*]

Cora: Yeah.

Windy: So, when I think about looking at these beliefs or attitudes, I think what I say is that both your what I call rigid attitude, which is the must, and the flexible attitude, which is the anti-must, if you like, that they both start off with a common core, which is your desire, which is, 'I really want to be clear and helpful to this client,' right?

Cora: Hmm-mmm [*yes*].

Windy: Now, one route goes, 'And therefore I have to,' and the other route goes, 'But I don't have to.' But they both have the desire. And, so, you're either anxious or concerned because of your desire. Now, the question I would ask you is do you think being anxious or being concerned is going to help you to concentrate more in the session?

Cora: Well, concerned is definitely more helpful. Yes.

Windy: Right. So, what I'm saying is you have a choice. Don't give up the preference because that just shows that you're a caring, professional person who wants to be helpful; that you'd like to be able to help and you'd like to be able to be clear and you'd like to be able to put it all together as quickly as possible. Then your choice is: 'And therefore I have to', 'But I don't have to.' That's your choice.

Cora: Yeah. ... [*Pause*] So, then, the Cora client comes in. So, when I don't have to,... the thing is then I won't have a successful practice and then I won't have...

[Although I have explained the fact that rigid and flexible attitudes begin with the same preference and it is this preference to be competent that will motivate Cora and not her rigid attitude, it is clear that I have not gotten my point across.]

Windy: Oh right. And, so, when you do have to, you will have a successful practice, right?

Cora: Yeah.

Windy: You can advertise yourself as 'The Anxious Therapist'. 'Come get great results from the anxious therapist'.

Cora: That's great. I'm going to write that down.

Windy: Yeah. But there is a serious point here and that is maybe you do need to accept but not like that whether you're anxious or concerned at the beginning of your career, maybe you're not going to be as effective as you will be towards the middle and towards the end of your career.

Cora: … Yeah.

Windy: It sounds like you're demanding that you be effective straightaway.

Cora: Yeah. … Kind of. It's just absorbing it right away and just applying, but I can't.

Windy: Well, yes. I mean, it is important to absorb something complex like REBT. I wonder whether the best way for you to absorb it is to be rigid or flexible.

[*The flow of the conversation gives me another opportunity to make my point about the differential effects of a rigid attitude and a flexible attitude.*]

Cora: Flexible. I'll take flexible.

Windy: Well, then, if you put it all together, how would it sound? Let's summarise where we've got so far today.

Cora: Yeah. So, I would really like to help my client and be clear in my approach, but I don't have to and, if I stay flexible and accept that I'm not as good as maybe later on in my career, I will feel concerned in session and that'll be more helpful for me to learn.

[*Cora's summary is accurate.*]

Windy: Yeah, and I would say that, in a way, one of the things practically that you can do is to be focused on one thing at one time.

Cora: Hmm-mmm [*yes*].

Windy: Which you've done in the motivational interviewing. You've actually had that success experience.

[*Here I draw upon the success experience that Cora had in the past when learning motivational interviewing.*]

Cora: Hmm-mmm [*yes*].

Windy: And it may well be that REBT is a little bit more complicated, but I can't imagine it's going to be that much more complicated. So, if you take, from your motivational interviewing experience, the idea that the way you helped yourself there is to focus one thing at a time, if you add that to the REBT idea that obviously you want to be as effective as you can as quickly as possible, but you don't have to be; you're learning.

Cora: Hmm-mmm [*yes*], right.

Windy: If I believe that becoming anxious would make you a more effective therapist, I'd say keep your musts, it's good for your clients. No good for you, of course, but they're great for your clients.

[*Here I am making another attempt to cast doubt on Cora's view that her demand to be a competent therapist will lead her to be a competent therapist.*]

Cora: Yeah. It's not helpful because I've seen it – my mind just goes blank a little bit.

Windy: OK. So, the questions is let's suppose, then, that you're in session and you start to find out that you're starting to get a little anxious. Now, I know it's difficult to stop in the middle of a session to do that, but let's imagine that you were going to stop and you were going to talk to yourself at that point. Now, what would you say at that point?

Cora: … [*Pause*] Remember to stay flexible, remember you don't have to get everything right. Focus on the one thing, whatever that one thing is, but just focus on that.

Windy: Right. Now, how does that sound to you?

Cora: It sounds… right, like I can apply that. It makes total sense and it's not that I'm getting so anxious that I'm completely losing it. I mean, I think I can talk to myself.

Windy: But it means giving up one thing. I wonder if you're prepared to give it up. Do you know what the one thing is?

Cora: The demand?

Windy: Well, no. The picture of yourself being hugely effective right from the start.

[Often novice therapists have a myth that it is possible to be effective as a therapist right from the start and that others can do this even if they can't.]

Cora: Right. ... Yeah. I mean,... yeah, I think I just need to picture myself learning as good as I can instead of getting it right already; that I am, 'Look, I'm learning. This is what I'm learning right now.'

Windy: Yeah, and you mentioned supervision. You got supervision from the motivational interviewing?

Cora: I didn't get it for that specifically. It's more of a general supervision.

Windy: And do you tend to learn from supervision? Do you find supervision a beneficial thing?

Cora: Yeah.

Windy: And are you getting supervision for your REBT?

Cora: I'm not but I will look into that.

Windy: Right. And do you think that would be helpful to you?

Cora: Yeah. Yeah.

Windy: Because otherwise you've got this idea, 'I've got
                to be effective straightaway. I have to know what
                to do and I've got to do it without supervision.'

Cora: Well, when you put it that way, it's really funny.

Windy: That would make anybody a nervous wreck, I
                think.

Cora: Totally. Welcome to my sessions.

Windy: Listen, you can always practise irrational emotive
                behaviour therapy. I don't care.

*[As I know that Cora has a sense of humour, I am using
humour here to underscore the point that her demand that she
has to be effective straightway without supervision is as she
says 'funny'.]*

Cora: Yeah, I will, opening a new branch.

Windy: Yeah, a new branch of the REBT. Now, is there
                any element of this that you want to focus on that
                we haven't yet discussed or are you good to go?

Cora: … You know, I think I'm good. I think that's been
                just really helpful. It's a good reminder for me to
                remember that I am a learning REBT therapist,
                even though I have experience with other things,
                but that's just what I decided to learn now and I'm
                just not doing it perfectly from the start.

Windy: Yeah. You know what, neither am I and I've been
                doing it since 1978.

Cora: Well, I don't believe that, I'm sorry.

Windy: It's true. Yeah, it's true. Probably made a few errors tonight – people with their competency checklist saying, 'Oh, he did this and he didn't do that. No, that's not good.' Well, you know, it's good enough and maybe that's what we're striving for initially: to be good enough.

Cora: Yeah, right.

Windy: But without the must.

Cora: Hmm-mmm [*yes*].

Windy: OK. Thank you very much for talking with me.

Cora: Thank you.

Windy: OK then, thank you.

14

Helping the Person to Take Pressure Off Her Son and Herself

Windy–Komal Interview on 22/02/21
Time: 10 minutes 49 secs

Windy: OK, Komal, what problem can I help you with today?

Komal: Oh yes, so my problem right now is I think I'm being too harsh on my child because of schooling, school pressure, study pressure, whatever way. It's not that I expect too much out of him, no I don't, but I don't know. I don't know. I'm being very... bad with him and it has affected our relationship. I won't say he hates me, but, rather than spending quality time, we're always either studying and then I'm so drained out that I don't want to spend quality time.

Windy: OK. Well, let me just ask you a few questions, if I may, to get a context, OK?

[Even though these are very brief conversations, I like to put the problem in context]

Komal: Yeah.

Windy: How old is your son?

Komal: Eight.

176

Windy: Do you have any other children?

Komal: Yes, I have a younger one, he's four

Windy: A boy or girl?

Komal: Boy.

Windy: Boy, OK. And do you have a partner or husband?

Komal: Yeah.

Windy: And is your husband hard on your son?

Komal: On me?

Windy: No, on your son.

Komal: No.

Windy: OK. So, give me an example of you being, what you said, too harsh?

[*Starting with an example of the problem is routine in any therapy format in REBT. An example will often bring the dynamics to light.*]

Komal: I mean, I can give you an example from last week only. We had exams and at the last minute the teacher changed the thing that was supposed to come in the practical. So, we were sitting the whole day and we were sitting until one at night just to finish the chapter.

Windy: Sorry, your son was sitting until 1 at night to finish a chapter?

Komal: I was sitting with him.

Windy: Right, OK. So, you were sitting with him.

Komal: Yeah, until one.

Windy: How long were you sitting with him for?

Komal: Oh, I think for a good five hours.

Windy: Right, and what was the difficulty?

Komal: The difficulty was that I feel that it's not that he was not understanding. We had to finish it because next day we had our presentation. So, we couldn't afford to leave it. So, I thought it was too much pressure and, of course, when I do that, you kind of get really rude in behaviour, as in I do tend to shout.

Windy: Wait a minute, when you say 'our presentation', you were making a presentation with him?

[*My view is that 'our presentation' indicates that Komal is overly invested in her son's schoolwork at least in this example.*]

Komal: No, I was trying to prepare him for the chapter, not making a presentation.

Windy: Right.

Komal: Just to clear out his concept.

Windy: Right, OK. And what was your goal? What's your goal about this?

Komal: So, that he understands the concept so that, if the next day the teacher asks him anything, he should know.

Windy: OK, I wasn't being clear. What's your goal in bringing the problem to me to change? What do you want to achieve?

Komal: I just want to be a bit more laidback.

Windy: So, if you were laidback at the time, if you were able to bring your laidback self to this example, what difference would you have made?

[*The goal of being laidback is rather vague so, I encourage Komal to be clearer on this matter.*]

Komal: First of all, I wouldn't sit until 1 with him. I wouldn't sit for a stretch of five hours with him. No, I wouldn't, because that is even pushing him away from studies.

[*Komal is giving me the absence of behaviours as her goal. I respond by asking for the presence of a behaviour as a goal.*]

Windy: Right. So, how long would you have stayed with him before?

Komal: Maximum I would say I would have stayed for an hour.

Windy: An hour.

Komal: Yeah.

Windy: And, so, you stayed for five.

Komal: Five.

Windy: And you would prefer to stay with him for one, right?

Komal: Yeah, maximum.

Windy: OK. So, what's the purpose of the extra four hours?

[Having got Komal's behavioural goal, I ask her what purpose the extra four hours served.

Komal: I don't think it served any good purpose.

Windy: No, it probably didn't as a result, but, at the time, you were influenced by something which led you to stay there. What do you think you were trying to achieve by the extra four hours?

Komal: I was trying to make him perfect in doing that chapter.

Windy: You were trying to make him perfect? Right. And you say that you don't have high expectations of your son?

Komal: Basically, I didn't want him to leave anything in the chapter, the reason being because I thought, if tomorrow the teacher would ask him whatever she might ask him from the chapter, because the teacher said, 'You should be thorough with the chapter,' so I said, 'If we leave something and she might ask something that is a part of the chapter and we have not done it, then all that hard work would go to waste, whatever time we have spent. So, it is better that we should do everything.'

Windy: So, your idea is that, 'I'm going to spend five hours over this just in case the teacher asks my son something which he can't answer, because, if they ask him something that I can't answer, the whole of our time has gone to waste.'

Komal: Yeah.

Windy: 'One wrong answer means the whole of our time together has gone to waste.'

Komal: Yeah.

[*Komal is showing black and white thinking here, 'Either my son is thoroughly prepared and can answer everything or all our hard work has gone to waste'. In REBT, black and white thinking stems from rigid/extreme attitudes.*]

Windy: Now, when you step back and you think about what you've just said, what do you think about it?

Komal: I know I'm wrong. I'm so wrong.

Windy: Well, wrong in what sense?

Komal: ... Now, when I look at it in hindsight, I feel that... he could've actually picked up things what I wanted him to do in way less time and I wouldn't have bothered about doing the whole thing. It's not the end of everything. He's just eight years.

[*When she stands back, Komal realises that it is 'not the end of everything' which I see as a non-awfulising attitude. As soon as she does so, she is able to put things in a healthier context as evidenced by her saying that her son is only eight years old.*]

Windy: It's not the end of everything, that's right, and would it be the end of everything if he couldn't answer a question?

Komal: No.

Windy: Right. So, I think what you're doing is you're actually adding to the work the idea that it would be the end of everything if he doesn't know the chapter perfectly and it would be the end of everything if his teacher asked him something that he couldn't know.

[*What drives Komal keeping her son up till 1 am is her awfulising attitude.*]

Komal: Right.

Windy: Now, if you took 'the end of everything' out of that and replaced it with something like 'it would be' what? What could you see it as?

Komal: … I mean, it's OK, we all learn from our things. I mean, what I have figured out is that it's OK. I don't care if he doesn't get full marks. I don't care if he can't answer.

Windy: No, don't lie to yourself because you'd prefer him to get full marks. You're lying to yourself.

[*I am endeavouring to help Komal come up with language to represent a non-awfulising attitude, language that takes into account her preference. However, she brings up another facet of the issue and I go with that. I would have preferred to finish the non-awfulising piece of work first and then make the shift.*]

Komal: The kind of effort I do put in I do try, but, seriously, that's not my expectation.

Windy: No, but what about your expectations of yourself? What are your expectations of you in preparing your son? You may not have the expectations of yourself, but what are your expectations about you, Komal, when you teach him things?

Komal: I expect him to do well.

Windy: So, 'When I teach him, I expect him to do well.'

[My sense is that Komal's rigid attitude is related to herself when she teaches her son.]

Komal: Yeah, when I teach him.

Windy: Yeah. 'When somebody else teaches him, then he's allowed to make mistakes, but, when I teach him, he's not allowed to make mistakes.'

Komal: I agree, yeah.

[Komal's agreement shows me that I am on the right lines.]

Windy: Well, are you happy with that philosophy?

Komal: Yes, I've got it.

Windy: But are you happy with that philosophy? Do you want to change that philosophy?

Komal: I'm not happy, no.

Windy: What do you want to change it to?

Komal: That... I need to bring down my expectations. I cannot do that.

Windy: 'When I'm involved, I'm going to try my best, within a set time, so that I feel that I'm doing well and to see if my son will do well, but, when I'm involved, I don't have to make him be able to do things perfectly. He's allowed to make mistakes whoever teaches him.'

[*Komal is rather vague in articulating a new philosophy so. I voice one based on the work that we have done in the session.*]

Komal: I agree.

Windy: Right. Now, if you really went and practised that philosophy, what impact do you think that philosophy and your behavioural change will have on your son?

Komal: I think I'll be more laidback, I'll be more cool in my head, I will not push him, what I'm doing right now.

Windy: Well, yeah, but you might still encourage him but within a boundary. You see, you haven't got a boundary.

Komal: Yeah.

Windy: I'm pretty sure if he hadn't got it after five hours, you'd have gone to six hours and seven hours and things like that. But, if you say, 'Look, we're going to do this for an hour and, in that hour, I'm going to do my best and I'm going to try to get him to do his best, but neither of us have to succeed.'

Komal: Right.

Windy: 'But the hour would be spent well educationally and the hour would be spent well as mother and son; we'd be getting on better with that philosophy.'

Komal: Right.

Windy: Because at the moment I think on neither front are you doing that well with your idea.

Komal: I'm not.

Windy: That's right.

Komal: I'm not.

[Here I show Komal that a flexible attitude will help her take the pressure of herself and her some and will probably result in them having a better relationship on such matters.]

Windy: But don't give up the idea that within a structure you're not going to try your best so that he can get the most out of something, but give up your demand about that and stick with sensible time limits, because, if you don't, you're going to go over.

[I also stress the importance of having a sensible time structure and keeping to it.]

Komal: Right.

Windy: Now, do you think you'll be able to put that philosophy into practice?

Komal: I'm going to do that. Thank you.

Windy: Good, that's what I like to hear.

Komal: I'm going to do that.

Windy: Determination. Good, OK, let's get the group's feedback.

15

Helping the Person to Accept that the Universe Does Not Have to Grant Her Righteous Request about Her Mother

Windy–Shama Interview on 01/03/21
Time: 14 minutes 11 secs

Windy: Hi Shama, what's your understanding of the purpose of our conversation today?

Shama: I'm expecting to get some help about a specific problem that I've been struggling with for a while.

Windy: OK, what's the problem?

Shama: I'm experiencing a lot of, I'm not sure if it's anger or if it's a lot of frustration, but probably a mixture of these things with my mother, who has currently been living with me for the past two months. So, yeah, that's where I am.

Windy: So, what's your dear mother been doing or not doing?

Shama: Yeah, well, I think that's an interesting question for her. So, we have very different personalities and we have very different approaches to things. So, she's an Indian mother who's been a

186

homemaker all her life and so, for her, her life revolves around caretaking. And, for me, that becomes a lot of boundary interference and a lot of coming into spaces that I don't need her to be in anymore, and that's where a lot of our conflicts come up from. So, I get very angry or frustrated and then it's followed up by guilt because I am being the bad daughter to my mother when she is trying to help me.

Windy: Have you got a specific example that would bring the issue to the fore?

[As is typical, early on I ask for a specific example of the nominated problem.]

Shama: Sure. So, today in the afternoon the agreement was for me to make lunch – we had decided upon that – but, despite me going ahead with my plan, being as it was agreed upon, she would still be around, she'd be hovering in the kitchen, 'Do you need me to do something? Let me do this for you. Let me make it easier. You need to take a rest. Why don't you do this? I'll do it.' So, that sort of constant wanting to be around and make things easier actually makes it much harder for me.

Windy: Sure. And how does anger help?

Shama: It doesn't help at all.

Windy: Right. By the way, is it healthy anger or unhealthy anger, would you say?

[Shama is familiar with REBT so I ask her an REBT theory-driven question which I am sure she will understand.]

Shama: I'm pretty sure it's unhealthy anger.

Windy: What gives you that impression?

Shama: Because there's a sense of seething inside.

Windy: A sense of seething?

Shama: Yeah.

Windy: Wow, OK, right.

Shama: And it's almost like I have this feeling of wanting to yell and be aggressive just to be able to make my point, which I know doesn't help at all.

[Shama has told me that she experiences an internal sense of seething and she feels like yelling and being aggressive towards her mother. These are all signs of unhealthy rather than healthy anger.]

Windy: OK. Do you ever yell and are aggressive?

Shama: Interestingly, only with my mum.

Windy: OK. Alright. So, what's your goal in bringing this topic to me today? What's your goal?

Shama: I want to be able to understand that this is who she is as a person and she's not changing, so, if I can rework my expectations around her, it will be more helpful.

[When I ask for her goal, Shama responds by telling me about what attitude she wants to acquire not how she wants to feel so I ask her about this below.]

Windy: What about your feeling of unhealthy anger? What do you want to do about that?

Shama: Move to healthy anger. Be irritated but not unhealthy anger.

Windy: Have you ever had the experience of moving from unhealthy anger to healthy anger before?

[Single-session thinking is guiding me here. If I can help Shama to identify a situation where she has successfully moved from unhealthy anger to healthy anger, I can encourage her to apply these salient points to her current problem.]

Shama: … *[Pause]* Maybe what I can relate to is my anger that used to be there around traffic-based situations.

Windy: Traffic?

Shama: Yes. I've come to a space of not getting bothered too much or understanding that me doing anything does not change any of the traffic issues around.

Windy: What attitude did you change to enable you to get that solution?

Shama: Well, to remind myself that I can't control it and all I'm doing, when I get angry, is hurting my own self or impacting my driving skills.

Windy: Alright, so, you reminded yourself that you can't control the traffic, you reminded yourself that, when you get unhealthily angry, you don't help yourself. And what about your demand? Did you change your demand?

Shama: Yes, that people don't really have to have a better driving sense because I want them to have it.

[*So Shama used the following salient points to hep her move from unhealthy anger to healthy anger about traffic: a) reminding herself what she can control and what she can't control; b) unhealthy anger doesn't help her and c) showing herself that others don't have to be the way she wants them to be.*]

Windy: OK. Well, why don't you apply that to your mother, see how it sounds?

Shama: I've been trying that but it's almost like in my head I'm saying, 'But she needs to understand. Why can't she get better?'

Windy: Well, and then what did you say in response?

Shama: … That she's not obligated to do it for me.

Windy: Yeah, but you see how your tone goes down? When you were saying, 'But she needs to do it,' it went up and then, 'but she's not obligated to do it for me,' it went down.

[*The tone of Shama's voice indicates that her energy is with her rigid attitude towards her mother not the alternative flexible attitude.*]

Shama: Yeah.

Windy: Are you giving this special status? I mean, do you find it easier to accept the fact that the traffic doesn't have to be the way you want it to be as opposed to your mother doesn't have to be the way you want her to be? Are you making your mother a special exception?

Shama: Yes, because, to some extent, I feel like, given the intimacy of our bond, I should be able to get her to a better space.

Windy: OK, so, if you had an intimate bond with the traffic, you still might be angry with the traffic.

Shama: I guess.

Windy: Yeah. You see, what you're doing is you're saying, 'Under certain conditions, I don't have to get what I want and these conditions are when it's traffic and it's really not so close and intimate with me. But, when things are close and intimate with me, particularly if it's my mother who's close and intimate, therefore the universe has to make a special adjustment for me and make sure that I do get my demands met.'

[*During this part of the conversation it becomes clear that Shama is adding certain conditions to her demand about her mother which are not present with the traffic – the closeness and intimacy of the bond between herself and her mother.*]

Shama: Yeah. Yeah.

Windy: OK, well, where's the evidence that the universe is going to make special exception for Shama?

[*Note that here I don't ask Shama to examine her demand towards her mother but the idea that the universe is going to make a special exception for her. Doing this work first will make it easier for her to examine her demand towards her mother.*]

Shama: None at all. In fact, there's only contrary evidence right now.

Windy: That's right, and the contrary evidence is what?

Shama: Is that she is going to continue doing what she has always done. She's probably going to continue being the person she's been.

Windy: Why?

Shama: … Probably because she doesn't see the need for change.

Windy: Well, what I say is because her behaviour is geared to her thinking and not to your thinking.

[*I often make this point when working with a person who has difficulties with other people.*]

Shama: Yeah, yeah.

Windy: Right?

Shama: Yeah.

Windy: Now, what do you think I mean by that?

Shama: Is that she is responding to her own goals and priorities and thinking and what she wants in a situation and not from mine.

Windy: Right. So, now you've got the interesting conundrum of, 'How do I change my mother's thinking?'

Shama: Yeah.

Windy: How are you going to do that?

Shama: ... I genuinely don't think that can happen because I've been trying these past two or three months. I've been really trying with peaceful conversations, with analogies, examples, sit down and talk about it, but I don't think that's happening.

Windy: But does she want to change?

Shama: ... I don't think so.

Windy: You see, you've been trying to change somebody's thinking who doesn't want to change. Now, do you want to change?

Shama: I need to.

Windy: That's not what I asked.

Shama: I want to. I want to.

Windy: Well, you sound a bit reluctant to me.

[*Shama has been investing her efforts in trying to change her mother's thinking rather than her own. When I ask her if she wants to change her own thinking she indicates reluctance, which I pick on and ask her about.*]

Shama: I think I'm still functioning from, if I'm asking for something better to happen, it shouldn't be this hard to get to that space and for me to have to make the less better alternative.

Windy: Because, if you accepted that grim reality, what would you lose?

Shama: … I'm not sure of what I'd lose, but I'm then signing up for a lifetime of these conflicting situations with her.

Windy: Well, you're signing up for a lifetime of asking yourself, 'How can I best change me in light of dealing with my mother?' rather than the lifetime of conflict based on your demandingness towards her.

Shama: Right.

Windy: But there is going to be a lifetime of some adversity, because the two of you have different priorities: you want one thing and she wants another.

[*Here I make the point that Shama is facing some kind of adversity whichever route she chooses: the adversity of dealing with changing herself to deal with living with a mother who wants different things from her or the adversity of conflict based on her rigid attitude.*]

Shama: Yeah.

Windy: And the question is how can you undisturb yourself while putting up with the adversity of living with your mother who wants different things from you? That's the challenge for you.

Shama: Right.

Windy: Now, unhealthy anger is only going to tip the balance into conflict.

Shama: Right.

Windy: Healthy anger, which recognises, 'Yes, this is a pain. I really wish my mother was more accepting and respectful of boundaries and I really wish that she did change her thinking, but, sadly, regretfully, unfortunately, she doesn't have to do so even though she's intimately connected with me. There aren't any special conditions in the universe.'

Shama: That's right.

Windy: Oh no, wait, wait. Hold on. I'm just getting a message from upstairs. Hold on. Wait a minute. Oh, you are! No, wait a minute, they are prepared to make special exception for you. Yes! Now, all you've got to do is take this[8] and really say, 'I want my mother to change, I want my mother to change,' rub it three times and I'm assured your mother will change.

[To help Shama accept grim reality in the sense that her choice is between the lesser of two 'evils', I introduce humour.]

Shama: Yeah.

Windy: Yeah what?

Shama: I mean, I so wish that that was for real.

Windy: Yes, so do I, because I'd do it every day with my hair. Every day I rub it three times and I say, 'I want special conditions. I do the rational emotive behaviour therapy Facebook group for nothing. Please, make special conditions for me.'

---

[8] I am referring to my Aladdin's lamp, which I use as a therapeutic prop.

[*In such circumstances, I tend to use a personal example that places myself in the client's situation. This shows that we are allies in this respect, which will help later.*]

Shama: It doesn't happen, yeah.

Windy: Well, you're not making a distinction between two types of specialness: one is you're special to you, but, two, are you special in the universe, Shama?

[*This is an important point. I am not suggesting that Shama surrender the idea that she is special to herself only that she is special in the universe.*]

Shama: … [*Pause*] No.

[*Shama continues to be reluctant.*]

Windy: Do you see how reluctant you are to accept that? Because, if you did, you'd say, 'Well, look, I'm not special in the universe, therefore it would be nice if the universe did show pity on me and change my mother for me, but, sadly and regretfully, it doesn't have to and it's unlikely that it's going to.'

Shama: Yeah, I'm still sort of stuck with that bit in my mind, that what I'm really demanding – I'm hesitating to say 'demanding' in my mind, I'm thinking what I'm asking for is righteous; it's rightfully a good thing to ask for.

[*Shama's rigid attitude here is, 'Because want I am asking for is rightfully good, I have to get it.'*]

Windy: It is a rightfully good thing to ask for. When I ask for hair, that's a rightfully good thing to ask for. It's not wrong. I'm not harming anybody.

Shama: Right.

Windy: But that's not the question. Just because you ask for something and you're right and righteous to ask for it, how does it follow that the universe has to give it to you?

[*This is an important for Shama to answer.*]

Shama: It definitely doesn't have to.

[*I am encouraged by Shama's answer and use her word 'definitely' to underscore this point as shown below.*]

Windy: Well, then, you'd better really definitely show yourself that and really get through to yourself, because I think you are saying, 'No, it's not much to ask for, and I'm right and, therefore, the universe has to give it to me.' That's one of the biggest things that we have to accept: that, no matter how special we think we are to ourselves and our loved ones, the universe or whoever's arranging for your mother to think the way she is, sadly it just is.

Shama: Yeah.

Windy: It's not going to take any notice of your righteous request, nor mine.

[*Again, I ally myself with the person.*]

Shama: That's right.

Windy: Right. So, why don't you sum up where we've got to so far?

Shama: The idea that it's fine for me to continue wanting this and to maybe even hope for it that at some point it may have an impact on her, but I can't be demanding for this and I don't want to keep demanding for it because it's not helping me and it's not helping my relationship with her. So, for me to move to continuing to want it and yet actually work with the practical reality and make changes with how she is, is going to be of better help.

Windy: Yeah, and also I would say don't worry if you find yourself making a demand, because that's not the problem. It's not the fact that you make it. The problem is that you perpetuate it; you don't stop it, you don't say, 'Ah, wait a minute, I'm demanding my mother be the way I want her to be. No, she unfortunately, regretfully doesn't have to,' and add some of those adverbs, because those adverbs will help you to recognise that it is sad, it is regretful, it is unfortunate, but it is what it is.

[This is a point that I frequently make in these conversations. The problem is not that Shama may begin by reacting from the position of a rigid attitude, the problem arises when she does not respond to this rigid attitude as quickly as possible. To soften the bitter pill I suggest that the Shama uses adverbs such as 'unfortunately' and 'regretfully' 'when showing herself that her mother does not have to comply with her righteous request.]

Shama: It is.

Windy: OK, let's see if we can get some of the group feedback.

References

Dryden, W. (2016). *Attitudes in Rational Emotive Behaviour Therapy: Components, Characteristics and Adversity-Related Consequences.* London: Rationality Publications.

Dryden, W. (2022). *Understanding Emotional Problems and Their Healthy Alternatives: The REBT Perspective. 2nd Edition.* Abingdon, Oxon: Routledge.

Ellis, A (1962). *Reason and Emotion in Psychotherapy.* New York: Lyle Stuart.

Ellis, A. (1983). *The Case Against Religiosity.* New York: Institute for Rational-Emotive Therapy.

Hoyt, M.F., Young, J., & Rycroft, P. (eds), *Single Session Thinking and Practice in Global, Cultural and Familial Contexts.* New York: Routledge.

Index

Lightning Source UK Ltd.
Milton Keynes UK
UKHW021843110621
385358UK00007B/266